MANAGEMENT OF HEALTH CARE SERVICES DELIVERY – A STUDY OF SELECTED TRIBAL SETTLEMENTS

ACKNOWLEDGEMENT

I express my deep sense of indebtedness to my research guide **Dr. D. Anand**, Reader, B.N.Bahaddur Institute of Management Sciences, University of Mysore, Mysore under whose constructive guidance and valuable suggestions the present study has been completed.

I am grateful to **Prof. B.Shivraj**, Chairman, B.N. Bahaddur Institute of Management Sciences, Mysore University, Mysore for his constant encouragement and co-operation.

It is pleasure to express my gratitude to **Prof. B.R. Ananthan** and **Prof. Aisha M Sheriff**, B.N. Bahaddur Institute of Management Sciences, University of Mysore, Mysore for the interaction and valuable suggestion. I am thankful to **Sri R. Mahesh** and **Smt M. Amulya** faculty of B.N.Bahadur Institute of Management Sciences.

I would like to thank **Mr.P.S.Prasad**, Liaison Officer, **Mr. Jagadish Bahadur**, Placement Officer, my fellow research scholars **Mr T.P.Mohankumar** and **Miss B.N. Kavitha** and all employees, Staff Members of B.N.Bahadur Institute of Management, University of Mysore for their help.

I owe my special thanks to Prof. A **Balsubramanian**, central University, Pondicherry for the encouragement during this study. I am overwhelmed with sincere feeling of indebtness to **Dr. K.V.A.Balaji.** It is my pleasure to acknowledge my gratitude to **Prof. Ranganath** for his valuable suggestions.

I would like to sincerely thank **Dr R. Girija Bai**. Scientist (Retd) CFTRI, Mysore for inspiring me for my research work. I take this opportunity to express my sincere gratitude to **Sri. Pradeep. R. Pandit Bangalore**, for encouraging me during the study. I am grateful to my friends, **Dr T.P. Renukamurthy, Sri Giridhar Deshpande,** who helped me to make this Ph.D. Program a successful one.

It gives me immense sense of gratification to place on records my profound gratitude and sincere thanks to each and every one of those who have helped me in this endeavor. I would like to apologize to those I do not mention by name here; I highly value their kind support.

I would like to thank my **Mother, Father, Wife, father-in-law** and **mother-in-law** for their constant encouragement during my research work.

VIVEK M BALSE

TABLE OF CONTENTS

LIST OF CHARTS

LIST OF MAPS

LIST OF DIAGRAMS

INTRODUCTION

Health – A national Perspective

India ranks seventh among the large countries of the world and it has the second largest population next only to that of China. Apart from its vast size and huge population what distinguishes India from other countries is it's geographical diversities and the multi ethnic, multi- religious and multi lingual character of the Society. This striking feature has attracted the attention of travelers and scholars from all over the world. While there have been thinkers who have scaled the pinnacle of philosophy, there are still pockets where animism is prevalent.

The study of the vast diversities, customs and racial characteristics can be and has been a subject of serious research for the anthropologists. It has a been a work of a lifetime for many of the anthropologists .One important segment of the Indian population is the tribal population of India living in different parts of the country. Probably, they are the original inhabitants of India. Even now, tribal population outnumbers the rest of the population, in certain parts of the country, and such areas, have been accorded a special status under the constitution.

In Karnataka state there are areas where the tribal population is predominant. These tribals are socio-economically backward. By and large they are at the lowest end of the social spectrum. They are continuing to lag behind on every dimension of development, be it, education, economic or healthcare, a situation, which demands a swift redressal.

The present study, which is being submitted, has focused its attention on the health condition of the tribals in the areas selected for the study, which presumably are reflective of their conditions in the other tribal areas of the country.

It is impossible to overemphasize the importance of health. "Health is wealth" is an age old saying. This was true yesterday, is true today and will be true tomorrow. The importance attached to the cause of health can be gauged traversing back into the history of ancient India. Right from the beginning, great importance has been attached to life and longevity. "Ayushman Bhava", "May you live long" used to be the blessing of the elders in our country.

A brief reference to the ancient system of medicines in India, which are still in vogue and relevant to this study are outlined below.

Ancient history of India is associated with the rich Vedic knowledge in all fields with respect to life and living. One of the impacts of the Vedic way of life is about the contribution made to the cause of Ayurveda (alternative system of medicine) in India There existed people who practised what was scripted in the health science branch of the Vedas underscoring the central factor of life – "Health". One such science related to health that has remained in practice even to date is the science of Ayurveda. The names of Charaka and Sushrutha are prominently associated with this system

Ayurveda comprises more than mere administration of medicine. Yoga, pranayama and dhyana are prominently associated with Ayurveda and have received scientific acceptance. They have become almost a rage among the Westerners.Unani is another system of medicine which was introduced into India by the Arab invaders. Probably the Arabs received this knowledge from the Greeks. Mogul history is replete with the contributions made by the Unani medical practitioners. A close examination of past Indian history will show that unani thrives as an alternative system of medicine in India even today.

If we look into the ancient Indian history it will reveal the fact that people looked for health care only in the alternative system of medicine, Ayurveda. This was but natural because they were not exposed to the allopathic medicine till the British started importing medicines and health care management services from the West. Perhaps the big invasion of Western medicine into India came with the discovery of Penicillin, an antibiotic to fight infectious diseases.

In the post independent period, commencing with the first five-year plan the government has laid emphasis on the development of the ancient systems of alternative medicine with required budgetary allocations. This, not only envisaged keeping ancient practice of Ayurveda alive but also to make it "affordable to the masses". Reviewing the practice and popularity of alternative system of medicine in India, we can state that this system, even today, is cost effective and employment oriented, giving relief to a lot of people directly and indirectly sustaining their livelihood.

With over three fourths of the Indian population living in the villages their closest source of medicine is the system of alternative medicine. Alternative medicine consists of ideas handed down from the forefathers of the families, which practice is carried on even today. Perhaps, one of the best examples here would be the use of turmeric powder for cuts and bruises as the best antiseptic application. No doubt, through conventional generics, allopathic medicines have made their way to the remote regions of our country.

There is no doubt that the western form of medicine has also contributed, on a massive scale, in disease management. Examples of controlling epidemics such as cholera, small pox etc shows its contribution has been remarkable. With the passage of time the western philosophy of health care management has digressed from the spiritual quest of "health for all "to corporate profiteering.

The opening up of the global economy under the WTO regime coinciding with the spread of dreaded diseases like AIDS, Hepatitis virus etc, catapulted the western mode of treatment from holistic level to global profiteering. Consequently, the western system of medicine became alarmingly expensive forcing the marginalized people of society to seek alternatives in health care.

The profiteering of the multinational drug manufacturing companies, the Intellectual Property rights (IPR) and patenting regime have played havoc with the people of developing and underdeveloped countries. IPR regime (Intellectual Property rights) has imposed restrictions on indigenous research and development, technological assistance and access to marketing of cheaper drugs. This has compelled the people of developing countries to seek alternative forms of medicine.

Health is not a mere absence of disease but has multiple dimensions. Good health also results in increased work output and productivity, which is the cornerstone of overall welfare. Poor health causes physiological distress, reduced quality of life, and physical disability and diminished work capacity. This causes increased societal cost. Poor health condition can be an important cause of capability deprivation resulting in unemployment and poverty. Therefore, both the infrastructure and its delivery of basic healthcare facilities have an overwhelming importance in enhancing a nation's manpower resource.

The proportion of people unable to afford basic healthcare has doubled in the last decade. One out of three people who need hospitalization and who are paying out of pocket are forced to borrow money or sell assets to cover expenses (Department of Statistics GOI).

Sound long-term development of social sectors such as education and health is vital for sustaining higher rates of overall economic growth (Dadibhavi and Bagalakoti 1994)

India's current health policy has its origins in the nation-building initiative at the time of Independence and in the thinking embodied in the Bhore Committee report. The Bhore Committee clearly modelled its vision for a public National Health Service on the one adopted by the United Kingdom (Bhore et al. 1946).

The high incidence of sickness (morbidity in technical terms) cuts into the budget of people in two different ways, i.e. they need to spend large amounts of money for treatment of disease and simultaneously are not in a position to accelerate production for generating additional income for meeting the expenditure.

Health care has become the utmost need of the day and can be ranked next only to food. The poor are particularly vulnerable in the present scenario. Providing health care for all citizens of India is a fundamental obligation, which the constitution of our country enjoins. Some of the factors, which contribute to good health, are the right to primary education, provision of free food in the schools for the poor and encouraging the adult education campaigns. The government needs to build the infrastructure that will create the necessary conditions for building such a sustainable environment.

Healthcare costs could be one of the primary reasons for rural indebtedness and poverty. Studies show that the poor spend a greater percentage of their earnings on health related expenditure. This happens because of the abysmally low hygiene practiced at their homes coupled with a lack of clean drinking water facilities, poor sanitation and low earning capacities, lack of state government health facilities, infrequent visits of social health workers and above all lack of literacy and prevalence of superstitious beliefs. According to National Advisory council 2006 "Medical expense is the single largest cause to push people towards bankruptcy and poverty in India".

The poor invariably suffer a loss of family income when they are sick. They have to bear a higher insecurity from illness resulting in a great deal of mental stress in the family. The number of Government health care centers and health care professionals is inadequate, especially, in rural areas where the actual need is higher. With this imbalance, the government is indirectly encouraging private medical practitioners to make a foray in unchartered areas where its own health care facilities are inadequate. Seeking quick recovery, the poor, therefore, go to private health care practitioners for medical treatment. The tragedy is that because of their ignorance, they are not aware of the quality of the medical treatment dispensed to them.

"A study conducted by David et al. (2002) "The poor still depend on the public sector for the majority of their health services, the private sector provides 79 percent of outpatient care for those below the poverty line, much of which is of low quality and provided by untrained practitioners".

Health of an adult individual in the rural area impinges directly on the income of the family. Therefore, health needs to be considered as an important component of progress and development of society.

Although the State Health Mission is chaired by the state chief minister and co-chaired by the health minister with the state health representation from the related

Departments, NGOs and private professionals etc. The WHO and professor Amartya Sen (2005) have a similar opinion that the health care index for India is far lower than that of some of the smaller under- developed countries. It would be worthwhile in certain areas to make frequent health checks in rural schools and colleges, and among agriculture workers and specially the rural women who bear the brunt of multitasking of domestic chores.

Further, there are wide differences in the health care facilities between rural and urban societies. The contrast between the rural and urban health care management services is growing at an alarming rate which when seen and compared leaves the observer shocked and dismayed. One observes with a sense of scepticism that urban India is trying to copy the western methods of high tech health care services giving rise to the idea that only the financially sound are entitled to good health care. If the divide increases on this pattern, the gulf between the haves and the have-nots will only increase. This eventually, will affect the social cost of medical treatment in urban centers because the mass of the people will exert pressure on availing themselves inexpensive government health care benefits.

Due to the growing population, rural demands for health care in India has become a distant dream for the underprivileged though the constitution guarantees the minimum healthcare for the poor. Some of the problems in rural health care are so alarming (high Infant mortality rate) that India is seen in a poor light in regard to health care benefits.

In this context, it will be worthwhile to quote a distinguished health care analyst Gaur et al. (2005) as to how the opening of the economy supposedly for accessing better health care has done more damage than good for the poor. Public spending on health is very low, stagnant at around 1 percent of gross domestic product (GDP) in spite higher incidence of malnutrition and diseases. "In the US it is 12.4 %, 6.5 % in Japan and 6.2 % in U.K. Such low spending puts India among the bottom 20 % of countries".

According to professor Sen. (1999), "poverty must be seen as the deprivation of basic capabilities rather than merely as lowness of incomes"

Both these factors are man made due to unequal distribution of the benefits derived in the process of economic growth. Merely increasing the gross domestic product to 8 percent makes itself irrelevant in the face of the lack of distributive justice. Studies show that the poorest of Indians forgo medical treatment 2-3 times more than the richest when ill.

In a developing country like India it is very important that substantial amount of funds are pumped into preventive and social medicine so that it takes care of health care services in rural areas in general and the tribal belt in particular.

In a study by Kennedy et al. (1996) income inequality was shown to directly affect the total mortality in a given population [$p<0.05$]. The same study measures income inequality by 'Robin Hood Index', which is that part of the income that needs to be redistributed from the rich to the poor to achieve economic equality. 1% rise in this index led to 21.7 excess deaths per 100,000 populations. This shows the profound effect income inequality has on the health of a population.

The hopelessness of the situation with regard to poor health care is all pervading. Malnutrition has made the health condition of the poor vulnerable even to common diseases. Income levels and deprivation have changed the contours of food habits from marginal intake to extremely low calorific values. There are reports that in the backward areas of Orissa state, the poor and the deprived live on shrubs and roots and other forest produce.

It would make sense for the government to help the tribals in self-employment schemes and construct the minimum required infrastructure for the sale of their produce. With this, their income capabilities will rise. Consequently, they may move from extreme deprivation to marginal livelihood. This, in itself, will raise the nutritional value of food intake, thereby restricting diseases that afflict them.

The history of health care management in India can also be viewed from the demographic point of view. While agriculture remains the main source of income, dependence on monsoon cannot be undermined. Inadequate rainfall results in resource crunch. For example, the year 2002-2003 saw a rain deficit of 19% for the whole country and 29% of the country faced drought under which 10% fall under severe drought condition problems (Badi et al).

The poor who live in villages with extreme dependence on monsoon and other natural resources bear the brunt of ill health. The patterns of land holding and size of the families make a tremendous difference in income generating capabilities of families. Heavy dependence on small acreage of land holding deprives them of nutrition and good health. Vagaries of monsoon also deprive them of steady income for maintaining themselves. This invariably drives them below the poverty line whose side effects are disease and death.

Though the above *analysis* seems systematic and logical yet complex issues continue to dog the administrative set up of the government in the proper management of the entire rural health care system. The government should strengthen its machinery in order to fulfill its commitment to health care management services. India's changing demographic statistics is imposing pressure on healthcare management but the government machinery has not been able to expand the infrastructure due to various factors. Though Governmental spending on Primary health Centers and sub units is on the increase, yet, people are not reaping the benefits. In spite of increased budgetary allocation by the government for rural health care management, the benefits do not seem to be reaching the poor owing to lack of monitoring agencies.

"About 85% of India's total health expenditure is financed by household out-of- pocket expenditure" (GOI website 2002).

"Analysis shows that public spending on health services including complementary expenditures on water supply and sanitation are just about 1.3 per cent of GDP. Given the low level of per capita GDP in the country, public health expenditure in per capita terms is abysmal. I hope to show the unequal distribution of resources. In India, Private health spending accounts for more than 80 percent of all health care spending, one of the highest proportions of private spending found anywhere in the world." (David et al 2002).

There is a rise in the government's resource commitment to the provision of health care services, which is evident with examples like constructing minimum facilities in local health care centers for meeting emergency such as nursing room for expectant mothers and good OPD (Out Patient Department) facility. Activity in vending medicine in rural health care centers is also on the rise. This is very crucial because none should be casual when dispensing medicine, which may affect the life of a patient. Educating patients through visual media like charts coupled with education and counseling centers regarding health and hygiene will go a long way in assisting the rural poor in social and preventive medicine. Wherever possible government has also set up facilities for dispensing alternative medicines so that the patient has a choice in availing himself of treatment.

All the programmes floated by government agencies are beset with overriding problems of high scale of unawareness, ineffective communication system, poor transportation facilities, to name a few. Consequently, health care programmes in rural areas have remained insensitive to the cause of medical aid of the poor. A visit to rural health care center for a practical assessment reveals the poor co-ordination of various activities. We have a long way to go in implementing the basic health care programme.

The following WHO Health report (2003) highlights the pathetic level of healthcare services in rural India. "Per capita expenditure on public health is seven times lower in rural areas, compared to government health spending for urban areas. The ratio of doctors to population in rural areas is almost six times lower than that in the urban population. Per capita expenditure on public health is seven times lower in rural areas, compared to government health spending for urban areas. Though the total spending on healthcare is 6% of gross domestic product (GDP), the state expenditure is only 0.9% of the total spending. People using their own resources spend the rest of it. Thus only 17% of the total health expenditure in the country is borne by the state, and 83% comes as 'out of pocket payments' by the people. This makes the Indian public health system grossly inadequate and under-funded. Only five other countries in the world are worse off than India regarding public health spending (Burundi, Myanmar, Pakistan, Sudan, and Cambodia)"

David (2002) analyses that “Indians who are hospitalized spend 58 percent of their total annual expenditures on health care. More than 40 percent of hospitalized people borrow money or sell assets to cover expenses”. Health care services are extremely expensive. Poorest of the poor struggle for survival every day. Those who are below poverty line and illiterate are more likely to procrastinate the visit to the medical practitioner and seek medical treatment. Consequently, the poor have to bear a higher cost of medical treatment as a result of delay. Poor quality of health care services in the rural area needs to be addressed urgently. “A study by ORG showed that in large parts of India health care services are very poor and not functioning effectively” (Shah 1989).

Holistic health care services encompass various fields that interact and bring out the best in patient care management. This system is what management experts call a “process driven system ” The processes symbolize the systematic functioning of health care services whose steps are as under:-

A. Diagnosis of the diseases

B. Laboratory test

C. Medical prescription

D.Counseling and follow-up.

While discussing management of health care services delivery it is very essential that the fundamental three-part operations are kept in mind in nursing the patients back to good health. They are as under: -

1. **Human resource development** - diagnosing the disease by health care professionals.
2. **Infrastructure** – Building Equipment and Laboratory.
3. **Drugs and its implication**- (pharmaceutical products) -To regain and stabilize the health condition.

Human Resource development

All professionals, once inducted into any stream of activity require training and development. Human resource development can be the process of introduction to a professional, as to how one needs to work in one's respective field. Training and development activity for a professional in any field is reinforcing and upgrading further skills to one's existing level of knowledge. Frequent exposure to exchange of ideas helps in understanding various factors that one may not be aware of. Programmes such as Continuous Medical Education (CME) for doctors expose them to advanced techniques in their respective speciality. Seminars, conferences and symposiums are platforms for debating, discussing and coming to consensus on disease management. Professional bodies like Indian Medical Association (IMA) and various periodicals encourage doctors to participate in exchanging views in the field of medicine. With the above assistance to medical professionals in exchanging and acquiring further skills it is assumed that treatments given by doctors are of the latest development in medical science.

Infrastructure

It is not uncommon to observe in cities hoardings and boards of hospitals claiming to have world-class infrastructure facilities catering to all fields of medicine. These privately run hospitals, no doubts, have facilities but the usage of them comes at a price. Normally, people below certain income levels do not venture into utilizing this world-class facility due to the cost involved. We are now trapped in conflicting situations about patient cure versus affordability. In view of this conflict, it becomes imperative for government health care machinery to establish infrastructure facilities such as diagnostic laboratories, consultation rooms, a minimum of clean waiting halls, drinking water facilities, clean sanitation and preferably, a unit dispensing medicine in all the health care centers. The problem arises in the maintenance of these buildings and in educating the people coming there to utilize the facilities with utmost care. Rural India is strewn with ignorant masses. Consequently, any amount of building good infrastructure facilities tend to get dysfunctional in a short period due to the apathy of the people at the helm of affairs in educating the masses on the value of facilities. We cannot squarely blame the ignorant masses on this score because exposure to literacy being at a minimal level they do not understand the concept of owning responsibility for good maintenance. Poverty and deprivation need not necessarily justify the reckless use of facilities at government health care centers as long as the monitoring personnel account for performance. It is because of this lack of a sense of responsibility that the health care centres are in a deplorable condition.

Hence it is very important to build the infrastructure facilities to help patients avail of quality treatment.

Drugs and its implications

It is generally presumed that medicine constitutes an integral part of the treatment. Today, even super specialists are very conscious about the optimal dose of a drug because of the side effects associated with its long-term usage. Many chronic diseases can be treated and advancement of diseases can be arrested by modifying the diet, life style and with less intake of drugs .In effect, to a great extent it is true that the underlining factor for extensive usage of drugs is uncontrolled vending of drugs without medical prescriptions. India has become the destination for testing new drugs in view of its massive market. Many drugs manufacturing companies have seen India as a massive profiteering center. In view of this, drug companies have escalated prices so alarmingly that they pinch even the pocket of rich.

It would be worthwhile for the government to step in and manufacture critical drugs at affordable prices. In fact, an action of this nature will ensure that the drugs reach to the rural poor because they are the section who are in dire need. A nation that is healthy reduces the social spending for basic health care and this saving accrued can be invested in more facilities in rural health care management. Government's initiatives in manufacturing critical care drugs at affordable prices will simultaneously dampen the prices manufactured by private companies.

The role of the essential medicines takes the center stage especially when patients are hospitalized. For example, a patient who has met with an accident and hospitalized is administered drugs as part of the treatment. This process during treatment in the hospital cuts further into the pockets of people.

Many are not aware of the quality of service in backward areas of India of the state managed hospitals. Statistics reveal that the conditions are very grim. It is here that the government must take proactive steps to strengthen rural healthcare management because continuous apathy in this regard may have disastrous effects.

A very unnerving factor today, is the high prices of even generic drugs. In reality this need not be the case as drug companies profit in volume sales .Yet, the insatiable appetite for profit keeps these prices high. As all drug companies have a share holding pattern in the public participation their prime concern has become the dividend declaration. Unfortunately, the WTO regime instead of lowering the prices of medicine has encouraged restrictive trade practices through IPR and patenting.

The philosophy of the globalization was to ensure "medicine sans borders" but unfortunately free trade has imposed a lot more restrictions than the previous GATT agreement into movement of medicine to the poorest of the poor in the world.

Speaking on the diseases of the poor Jeffrey D Sachs, (2007) Director of the Earth Institute of Columbia University, said "they are hellish infections whose combined impact of disease, disability and death rivals the impacts of AIDS, tuberculosis and malaria, yet they are far less known, partly because they are diseases that afflict only the poor in the tropics".

In this context of escalating drug prices it is important for us to observe the importance of Ayurveda, which has a rich tradition of manufacturing medicines at affordable prices. Ayurvedic treatment does not discriminate between the rich and the poor nor does it exhibit class distinctions.

Health is a function, not only of medical care but also of the overall integrated development of society-cultural, economic, education, social and political. Each of these aspects has a deep influence on health, which, in turn, influences all other aspects. Hence, it is not possible to raise the health status and quality of life of people unless such efforts are integrated with the wider effort to bring about the overall transformation of a society (Basu 1993).

Effective and timely reach of health care benefits is a precursor to poverty reduction. Sickness compromises the earning capacity of the rural families. Following quote from WHO has this description in it.

"This year's World Health Report comes at a time when only a decade is left to achieve the Millennium Development Goals (MDGs), which set internationally agreed development aspirations for the world's population to be met by 2015. These goals have underlined the importance of improving health, and particularly the health of mothers and children, as an integral part of poverty reduction" (WHO 2005).

Tribal Health Care System

Mahatma Gandhi, father of the nation, coined the word Girijans for tribals in India meaning, children of forest God. The tribal welfare has been a concern in India and across the globe alike. United Nations had declared 1993 as the International Year of the Indigenous Peoples.

The tribal population of India (67.6 million) is larger than that of any other country in the world. In fact, it is almost equal to the tribal population of nineteen countries with substantial tribal populations. Mynamar, with a tribal population of 14 million, has the second largest tribal population. India has a tribal population, which is much more than four times that of Myanmar and more than six times that of Mexico (10.9 million), which has the third largest tribal population in the world. The tribal population of India is more than the total population of France and Britain and four times that of Australia. If all the tribals of India had lived in one state, it could have been the fifth most populous state after Uttar Pradesh, Bihar, West Bengal ad Maharashtra. (Singh1993).

Tribals remain the most backward ethnic group in India despite the protection given to the tribal population by the Constitution of India on the most important issues like health and education. Tribal health and treatment are closely interrelated with the environment, particularly the forest ecology. Tribal populations, generally have poor health outcomes, because, often a healthcare delivery system does not cater to their needs. The mode of utilization of available natural resources often determines the long-term impact on health of tribals in India.

It is due to a combination of many factors that tribals continue to use their own model of health care products and health care delivery system in India. Principal factors among them are urban and rural divide, economic disparity, governmental neglect and illiteracy. This forced shift of the tribals from their environment, which they had co-habited for generations made them forego their traditional arts. It was also a dire necessity that in the absence of any modern health care system they had to use their own home remedies.

Post independent era witnessed displacement of tribal habitats in many parts in India due to infrastructure developments like roads, water irrigation, bridges etc. This forced shift of tribal habitat, as they had learnt to co-habit with environment for several generations, made them, forego many arts. One of the many important valuable arts that we lost, as a consequence in India is tribal medicine. Non-availability of herbs in their new area also contributed to degeneration of tribal medicinal knowledge. At the same time, helplessness during the health breakdown made tribals overtly dependent on the degenerated version of the tribal health care system. Most of the time, it is their strong immune system that helps them overcome minor ailments.

Many researchers have attempted to review the effects of the growing socio-economic inequality in Indian population and its effect on the healthcare system. Although government has exhibited a great degree of concern and tried to provide health care infrastructure to tribals, it appears that there has been little effort to identify the factors responsible for the difficulties in healthcare delivery in tribal society and its effect on the health of the tribal society as a whole. It is also a fact that though innumerable studies on tribals are made, a systematic knowledge about tribal healthcare system is very limited leading to many myths.

Dr A K Singh (1993) has brought out a voluminous book "Tribes and tribal life" which is a painstaking twenty years of study. He has examined the effects of planned developmental intervention in the tribals from 1961 to 1981. He has concluded that twenty years of intervention has not made any significant impact in improving the conditions of the tribals.

The health care policies in recent times were expected to improve the situation. Till date the situation remains the same. A study done by .Dr Nirmala

Murthy (2006) suggests that the poor still find it difficult to avail the health care services. ''Notwithstanding these policy level efforts, the two main impediments affecting our ability to reach services to the poor are: (i) corruption and (ii) negative attitudes of health staff towards the poor. Many studies have documented that workers extract money from the poor tuberculosis patients to give them a sputum cup, to provide them a bed at hospital, sometimes even to allow them to see their newborn babies".

It is an unequivocal opinion of many social researchers that good health and good society go together. But this is possible only when supportive components such as nutrition; economic conditions and education reach a certain level It is quite interesting to note that there exists a definite correlation between forests and nutrition in the context of tribals. It has been noted by many researchers that tribals living in remote areas have a better overall health status and eat a more balanced diet than tribal living in less remote, forest free areas. Many tribal groups use different parts of a plant for the treatment of diseases. There are a few time tested herbal medicines, knowledge of which is passed on down the generations in a few tribal families. It is worth considering to preserve this knowledge before it becomes extinct.

It may be mentioned that health related studies about tribals are limited. Among the available studies, many are fragmentary in nature without an adequate sample size and standard methodology. Many studies are written in the form of articles with glamorous outlook, which may fall short of giving a clear and complete picture.

The tribals are more backward not only compared with the general Population, but also compared to the Scheduled Castes, the other acknowledged backward social group with a constitutional protection. In fact, the conditions of tribals in post-independence India have, in many ways, worsened. This has been discussed in a special issue of Social Change entitled "Status of the Tribals in India (1993, vol. 2&3)". The tribals are the most adversely affected ethnic group due to the developmental projects of dams, factories and mines. While tribal population constitutes approximately 8 percent of the total national population about 40 percent of displaced persons due to developmental projects are tribals.

A disturbing dimension of the tribal habitat is the pace of commercial exploitation of the land resources where tribals lived for centuries. This range of land accounts for nearly 20 percent of the country's space with 8 percent of its population living on it. The tribal rights in basic resources such as land, forest and water in fact in the entire environment have been seriously eroded. This is due to the consequence of non-tribal peasants, traders, businessmen and other categories of aliens having moved into tribal land with the concept of profiteering commercial ventures. Rapid industrialization moves mooted by modern policy makers also has its share in it.

Prolonged denial of modern health care benefits to tribals has been an undisputable fact. Disparity coupled with illiteracy has paved the way for many chronic diseases including genetic abnormities. Chronic diseases like leprosy, malaria and typhoid are rampant in tribal areas.

Malnutrition, often is, a causative contributory factor for children and women to fall sick. Maternal and childcare is an important aspect of health seeking behavior, which is largely neglected among the tribal groups (Basu et al 1990)

Many studies show a gross deficiency of vitamin C and calcium in tribal populations. General insensitivity of society in general and governmental neglect in particular has resulted in poor health care reaching the tribals. Many studies in tribal areas have been done from a clinical and epidemiological perspective. There are yet other studies investigating their social life styles, cultural factors, mortality etc. But there are hardly any studies to suggest a comprehensive model to reach the benefits of modern health care systems to these areas.

It is but natural that tribal women and children are the most affected due to the social conditions and traditional practices in tribal societies. Tribal groups are isolated and maintain homogeneous social systems. They are also culturally very firm. Thus they develop their own health care system and understanding of disease along with medicines from plants, minerals and other natural resources. Many tribal groups have their magico-religious healthcare system. Innumerable studies have been done on the socio-cultural issues of tribal society including food, marriage systems, herbal treatment etc. but they are not focused on the actual basic health care need of the tribal society.

Health care professionals, medical equipments and basic infrastructure with laboratory facility are the basic components in a health care center to provide health care services to the tribals. Paucity of manpower, lack of infrastructure and medicine often make a poor tribal unable to get even a basic treatment facility. It is a matter of concern that while urban society benefits from a modern and preventive health care facility, the counterpart in tribal area does not even have an access to treatment facility.

A disease at an advance stage may require surgery under complete medical treatment. Therefore, complete health care would need surgical services as an inherent part of medical treatment. But due to the acute shortage of human resource and lack of adequate infrastructure tribals have to travel to distant places to avail themselves of surgery. Existing infrastructure in tribal areas is not equipped with surgical facility to handle even basic injuries and excisions. Some times, secondary surgical units are too far to reach from the tribal area and may land patients in life threatening situations.

Against this backdrop, it is interesting to note the observations recorded by Patti Chico, a British midwife, who travelled widely in tribal areas of our country. A paramedical staff from England, Patti Chico (2003), while appreciating many of the social disciplines practiced by the tribals, was equally concerned about their lack of access to modern heath care benefits. Patti Chico expressed serous concern about the need for surgeons in tribal areas. In a letter to her home Patti Chico wrote " I came to India believing that I could teach something to the health care workers of Sittilingi and have found myself truly humbled by the experience. I wish I could have given just a little to these people from whom I have learned so much".

Patti Chico later launched Rural Surgical Initiative (RSI) in collaboration with "Tribal India Health Foundation". Rural Surgical Initiative (RSI) was launched with the purpose of increasing the quality of surgical care in rural areas of India, beginning with tribal areas of South India.

The Foundation aims to fulfill the following under the RSI program:

1) Continue to collect and send surgical supplies, including sutures, pulse oxymeters, gloves, scalpels, etc. to partner tribal health initiatives.
2) Recruit surgeons from the United States on a voluntary basis to assist in providing basic surgical care at partner tribal health initiatives for a short period of time.
3) Secure funds for expansion and development of basic surgical facilities in tribal areas
4) Provide rural surgeons with education materials on the latest developments and methods in basic surgery
5) Ally with rural surgical groups in India to jointly increase the scope and standard of surgical care in rural India.

The Foundation invites individuals, organizations, and surgeons to take part in its organizational activities, which include: -

1) Collecting surgical supplies for partner tribal health initiatives
2) Volunteering to provide surgical services at partner tribal health initiatives for a span of around 2 weeks (surgeons only)

Health is a function, which goes much beyond medical care. Overall integrated development of social, cultural, economical, educational and mental conditions have great impact on health in general. Each of these aspects has a deep influence on health, which, in turn, influences all these aspects. Hence, it is not possible to raise the health status and quality of life of tribal people unless such efforts are integrated with the wider effort to bring about the overall transformation of a society.

It appears that the common beliefs, social customs and practices connected with tribal life have been found to be closely related to their pattern of treatment of diseases. Therefore, it is necessary to take a holistic view of all the cultural dimensions of the tribal life before the health of the tribal community is studied. For instance, in most of the tribal communities there is a wealth of folklore related to health. It is an important observation done in many studies that documentation of this folklore available in different socio-cultural systems studies that tribals lead their life in harmony with nature. Systematic collection of folklore may be very worthwhile and could throw light on newer approaches in shaping health care policy. (Hedge 1988)

Tribals of different age groups and gender would require a separate approach in health care. Cultural practices are the determinant elements for a tribal woman to access the education, medical care and other health resources. The cultural norms that particularly affect women's health are attitudes towards marriage, marriage practices, age at marriage, values attached to fertility and sex of the child, pattern of family organization, her status in the society, decision making capability and the ideal role demanded of women by social and cultural conventions (Kshatriya 1992)

The pattern of marriages in Indian society is largely governed by three important regulations, namely

a. Endogamy (marrying within the group of birth)
b. Exogamy (marrying out of the group)
c. Consanguineous or sapinda marriage. The regulation of consanguineous marriages does not permit marriages between two individuals related though a common male ancestor up to the seventh generation on the father's side, there is a greater incidence of consanguineous marriages specially among the populations of the southern States, Muslim groups, Parsees and various tribal communities (Basu 1985).

In many tribal communities, cross-cousin marriages are preferred and practised. The system of cross cousin marriage had proved to be beneficial to the females in terms of care and treatment at husband's place. It also avoided high bride price/dowry and maintained the property of the household intact.

While a tribal woman found a social comfort in the cross-cousin marriages, modern science does not support it due to serious side effects associated with progeny. Some of the proven undesired effects are Chances of abortions, miscarriage, stillbirth, and neo-natal death increase due to consanguineous marriages. Also, there is higher risk of infant and juvenile death, greater probability of child being born with physical and mental defects. Children born of consanguineous marriages are also more prone to infections.

Very little information is available on maternal mortality and some information can be found on infant mortality among tribal population.

Woman plays a significant role in the tribal society. The tribal woman from the forest procures all the family's need for food, Medicine, fuel and house building material. The woman plays a key role in providing basic needs for her family and hence most tribal economies are women-centric. The forest provides tribals with all their needs and tribals are economically dependent on it. Food is obtained from the fruits and flowers found in the forest. Tribals take up cultivation of vegetables during the non-monsoon seasons. Tribal medicine is usually made from extracts of roots, herbs and animals and sometimes minerals.

Rapid deforestation was witnessed in our country after independence due to urbanization. Deforestation has led to a chain of unfavorable consequences for tribals. The government has sought to increase its control over forests thereby making the life of tribals even more difficult. This has resulted in sacrificing the age-old practice of collecting forest produce from forest and making a living. The task of collecting fuel has become very difficult for tribal women due to appointment of agents for collecting forest produce. This has also adversely affected the livelihood of tribals.

This has resulted in decreasing incomes leading to poor nutrition. Wood is less accessible and hence collecting fuel has become a time-consuming task. With fuel collection itself taking up so much time, tribals are left with little time to earn wages. As government control over forests increases, hunting is also not possible. It is noticed that in the early seventies almost 20 percent of women were found to be participating in activities other than agriculture. All they were provided with were a few tin sheds in the forest area near by. But today less than 10% of tribal women are involved in activities other than agriculture.

One of the pertinent examples is that of the national park around Nagarhole forest in Karnataka. The Wildlife Protection Act (1972) has resulted in the tribals losing all rights to reside in the national park. This has led to mass evacuation of tribals from forests. Almost 32000 tribals living in and around the national park have been constantly on the move with no place to reside permanently.

Subsequently, the act was modified in 1988 and the area was adapted to 643.39 Sq. Kms. Due to this modification the tribals were able to live in some parts of the national park area once again. A consequence of this evacuation was that the indigenous system of medicinal practice of tribal was lost to some extent.

One more similar example would be about the Kabini river project in Heggaddevankote (H.D.Kote) in Karnataka. In this ambitious project by government of Karnataka 18 tribal Haadis (or settlements) were ousted to make way for the Kabini river project. None of these displaced tribals have received compensation of any kind.

Yet another relevant example is that of Taraka dam .The Taraka dam constructed in the early 70s again displaced two tribal Haadis without any compensation. Some were accommodated in tin sheds in nearby forest areas. In the new places they were unable to get the herbs they used as medicine. At the same time these tribal population were not given any health care facilities.

In most tribal communities maternal and child health care is non-existent. In several studies it was found that expectant mothers were neither inoculated against tetanus nor did they take any specific nutritious food during pregnancy. On the other hand, the expectant mothers in much of tribal society consume less food so that the baby is born small and delivery is easier.

In most cases poor intake of iron, calcium and vitamins was observed during pregnancy. Women continued consuming alcohol during pregnancy and also went on with their regular chores even during the advanced stages of pregnancy. Due to unavailibity of qualified medical practitioners in tribal areas, help of paramedics (Nurses/midwives) is sought only during a difficult delivery. Elderly women of the tribe handle most deliveries. Also it was observed that no specific precautions were taken at the time of delivery resulting in greater risk of infection to the infant.

There are some problems, which are specific only to the tribal community in India. Basu (1992). While a large number of these problems are inbuilt, a few of these problems have been imposed on them. This has proved detrimental to their health, overall development and progress. One of the ways to improve the health status of tribal women would be to develop health care systems for each tribal community, keeping in mind the specific needs and their associated health problems. Also efforts should be made to ensure the tribals' involvement in all the projects.

Basu (1992) made an analysis of the health status of the tribal women in India and he recommends following guidelines

1. Formulation of realistic development health plans based on needs as felt by tribal women of the specific tribal groups.
2. Need for promotion of nutritional and health education among the working, lactating and pregnant tribal women.
3. Healthy nutrition should be encouraged through the local produce and local recipes. The tribal women themselves, through a better utilization of their locally available cheap but nutritious food should fulfill their nutritional needs.

    - Development of poultry and fisheries are to be encouraged.
    - The local tribal women should impart health education with the guidelines provided by health functionaries.
    - The nutritional and health status of pregnant tribal women need to be improved by adequate intake of nutritious diet, including iron and minerals and also by hundred percent immunizations.
    - Tribal women in their advanced stage of pregnancy should be advised to reduce their workload and take adequate rest.
    - The habit of taking alcohol and drugs during pregnancy should be discouraged.
    - The children should be properly immunized, the harmful practices of discarding colostrums, delayed initiation of breastfeeding and complementary

feeds should be discarded and health education aspects should be properly explained to tribal women.

- Tribal girls should be properly trained as "dais"/nurses. Specific precautions need to be observed at the time of conducting deliveries at home; aseptic conditions need to be followed for cutting the naval cord.
- Primitive practices of parturition are to be discarded and necessary health education should be imparted to tribal nurses.
- Tribal nurses or “dais” should properly explain the maintenance of personal hygiene in connection with childbirth, abortion or menstruation in order to prevent the infections of the female genital tract.

A number of studies have revealed that regular counselling can bring out great changes in the health condition of tribals. The fundamental question is about trained human resource to be made available in tribal areas. A study was conducted by the Indian Council of Medical Research (ICMR’s Regional Medical Research Centre) Jabalpur, about the health problems of several tribes in Madhya Pradesh. The study reveals that certain inherited disorders such as Thalassemia and sickle cell anemia can be prevented through proper counselling.

But this observation of the advantages of mass awareness could not be translated into action due to the lack of trained health care professionals in tribal areas. A casual glance at the number of medical and paramedical colleges creates a sense of euphoria. The fact that nearly 15,000 new graduate doctors and 5,000 postgraduate doctors are trained every year makes it appear that an abundant number of medical personnel are being trained in our country.

However, a closer look reveals that most of the trained personnel prefer to provide their services in urban areas creating an unequal distribution of resources between the urban and the rural areas. This gap in the health care resources has been a serious concern as even bare minimum services are not accessible to the tribals. A Lot of reasons can be attributed to this incongruity.

In the hierarchy of rural public health facilities, Community Health Centres come first, Primary Health Centres next, and finally the subcentres. Each subcentre is expected to serve a population of around 5000. (WHO 2005)

Effective delivery of the local public healthcare in India is choked. Government programmes with independent planning and implementation operate with little or no coordination with the other programmes on the ground. At present, the availability of specialist and surgical services at the rural hospital level is very low. "According to a country wide facility sample survey in the year 2000, less than 30% community health centers (CHCs) had an obstetrician available; less than 10% had an anesthetist. Government spending on health is grossly inadequate at this point of time. It is around 1% of the GDP which is roughly one fifth of the total health related expenditure in the country. But the government has acknowledged this shortcoming. If the extra activities are to be managed within the same level of government spending it is clear that the services cannot be improved. Government is committed to spending 2-3% of GDP and this commitment needs to be fulfilled if these new plans have to succeed. Additional budgetary provisions must be made which has already been promised"(Abhijit 2005)

But the disappointment with the Union Budget 2007-08 has been the reduction in the allocation for the reproductive and child health programme, compared with the 2006-07 budgetary estimates, from Rs 1,765.83 crores to Rs 1,672.2 crores. This, despite the fact that India's infant and maternal health indicators are among the worst in the world. What's more alarming is the fact that what is allocated shows poor utilisation, as, between the 2006-07 budgetary estimate and the revised estimate, there is a decline of over 24%. In fact, allocation for child health has fallen for the second consecutive year -- from 0.55% in 2006-07 to 0.48%. In the 2005-06 budget, its share was 0.52%. By neglecting child health in favour of education, the government has once again failed to take a holistic view of the needs of children. The budget neglects two important areas -- child health and child development. Out of Rs 3,2958.33 crore promised to children of this country, education hogs a 72.4% share and development 16.65%; health gets 10.02% and protection 0.92%.(Haq–Centre 2007)

For instance, the incentives given to doctors and nurses to move to rural areas are not sufficient and they choose to be in urban areas. It is difficult to maintain understaffed health care centers in remote areas. Since these centers are not well equipped, people hesitate to use even the existing facilities in these health centers.

The tribal patients are at a great health risk due to the conditions in which they live. This is further aggravated by their exposure to extreme climate, poor housing facilities, their susceptibility to diseases and air water and soil pollution.

At the same time better medical facilities are available in the private health care centers located in taluk headquarters. However, these are not easily accessible to the tribal poor due to their high cost. This has increased the gap between the facilities available for the rich and the poor. Due to control of the private players in health care sector, the poor are denied good medical facilities.

Also, private health care services are concentrated in urban areas and the main motive is profit. Higher the payment better will be the services offered. A recent World Bank report acknowledges the facts that doctors over-prescribe drugs, recommend unnecessary investigations and treatment and fail to provide appropriate information for patients even in private healthcare sector. This report also points out the relation between cost and quality that is the bane of the private health care system. Sometimes, even though the services offered are excellent, the common man cannot afford them. (World Bank Report 2005) Thus the availability of health care services for tribals is influenced by socio-economic factors.

There have been a number of developmental works conducted by governmental agencies in the post independent era in our country. The impact of development programmes has been different on different sections of tribal population. The tribal woman has been in a more disadvantageous position compared to her nontribal counterpart. Although a small number of tribal women have taken advantage of education and the new opportunities for employment, majority of them still lead a pathetic life.

This is due to the fact that Development has had its drawbacks. Some of the negative effects of development are listed below. (Rajyalakshmi.et al 1993)

- The workload on women has increased considerably.
- With increasing use of modern agricultural equipments, women are marginalized in agriculture. This leads to their migrating to other areas as labourers.

- Due to greater government control over forests, women cannot profit much from the forests.
- Women are exploited in various ways. Some of the ways of exploiting women are as follows: -

    a) Due to the enactment of various acts such as Rural Land Ceiling Act, Tribal Land Transfer Act, etc, in order to purchase land from tribal poor non-tribal men marry tribal women just to avoid legal complications. Sometimes they get monetary benefits from the govt. also for marrying tribal women. However, such women may not get the status of a wife.

    b) Sometimes mine owners take away land for development purposes. No other land is given in exchange nor do these mine owners bother to rehabilitate the displaced tribals. Whenever a vacancy is there, they prefer to employ men rather than women who are the sole inheritors/owners of the land.

    c) In nationalized mines women are not allowed to work in the evenings & night shift. However, they are permitted to work in private mines but private mine owners prefer to employ men as women have to be given maternity benefits, rest shelters, equal remuneration and also crèches have to be provided.

    d) Voluntary retirement schemes are aimed at relieving women of their jobs. A woman may retire after 36 years and give her job to a man who will then continue with her PF account and get all the benefits.

    e) Tribal women often become easy targets for immoral trafficking.

    f) Rejas (women labourers) are sexually and socially exploited. Most of them are not married and parents do no not want to get them married fearing loss of income. Men also prefer to marry non-rejas.

Data available on tribal women suggests the following:

1. All tribal women are working women. Tribal women are overworked. They get up early in the morning and set out to find fuel. Then they fetch water, assist in agricultural activities, do household chores etc.
2. They are always paid lower wages than men even though the workload is the same on both.
3. Deforestation and development project have adversely affected tribal women.
4. Employers are always devising ways and means to lay off tribal women.

It is important to study the above-mentioned points to formulate any health care delivery system, as tribal families are matriarchal. In the eventuality of health break down it is the woman folk of tribal society who have to take a lead to avail of the health care facility. Emphasis on educating tribal woman would be a giant leap in the developmental programme of tribals.

A Case Study done by Jayalakshmi (2003) in Andhra Pradesh where tribal women were trained bears testimony to it. The above paper is an empirical study conducted in one of the International Tribal Development Agencies (ITDAs) of Andhra Pradesh. It took a look at the health care system provided to the nine mandals in the region through the World Bank IPP-VI project. In an attempt to make modern health care facilities available to tribals, women from the community were trained as Community Health Workers (CHW). They were given sufficient training so that they could provide basic curative services, health education and take preventive measures against diseases at the village level. The Community Health Workers (CHW) formed the link between the tribals and health care personnel.

They served a dual purpose of both providing health care and performing the role of building up rapport within the community. The Village Tribal Development Agency (VTDA) overlooked the activities of health care units in the area. This agency is, in turn, aided by the Village Health Committee (VHC) and Village Development Fund. The activities are meant to be implemented jointly by the Village health Committee and village development fund, which in turn encourages people to participate in its activities. The system has been developed in such a way as to ensure that it continues functioning effectively even after the government role is gradually reduced. It is commendable to note that the participation of tribal women led to success of healthcare programme.

Basu's (1993) extensive work in the field of tribal health care and the health problems of the tribal population can be summarized as follows: -

1. Deficiency of essential components in diet leading to malnutrition, protein calorie malnutrition and micronutrient deficiencies are common. Goitre of various grades is also endemic in some of the tribal areas.
2. Water borne and communicable diseases: Gastrointestinal disorders, particularly dysentery and parasitic infections are very common, leading to marked morbidity and malnutrition. Malaria and tuberculosis still remain a problem in many tribal areas, while the spectrum of viral and venereal diseases have not been studied in-depth.
3. High prevalence of genetic disorders mostly involving red blood cells: Genetically transmitted disorders like sickle cell anaemia, deficiency and different forms of thalassaemia are also common. All these defects lead to the early destruction of red blood cells and add to the overall anaemia.
4. Excess consumption of alcohol: The brewing of alcohol from Mohua flower and fruits has been practised traditionally. However, the switch over to commercially available liquor is likely to be a major threat.
5. Superstitions particularly related to health problems.

Need of the study

Although a vast body of knowledge about tribals has been accumulated under different branches of knowledge, it is always felt that the information on health care delivery is far from complete. India's health care system is driven by patient's demand. In nongovernmental health organizations, resources by and large are ploughed in, in response to patient's ability to pay and there is little incentive for quality care among staff workers. In Government health care centers efficient use of resources is not a primary consideration. This field being perpetually incomplete attracts more and more researchers to explore gray areas and to add newer dimensions.

It is interesting to note that the government taking great interest and building infrastructure periodically but the system is ineffective to deliver the value hence has a poor " customer perceived value". This aspect of poor health care delivery creates a need for the systematic study

"It may, however, be mentioned that (Tribal) health related study is found to be limited, most of the available studies fragmentary in nature without an adequate sample size and standard methodology" (National Commission for Women.1993).

"The data sources commonly utilized for such purposes are one or a combination of following: registration and surveys- both complete enumeration surveys and sample surveys. Administrative reporting also provides information in many cases .For informed decision making it is pertinent to check the coverage, reliability and timing of different resources". (Roy 2003)

In view of the poor health care infrastructure available in the tribal areas there is a need to survey the tribal environment to reason out the moderate to poor functioning of the value delivery system in Health Care

Most studies, which have been undertaken so far, are dealing with the reasons for poor health condition of Tribal-health but unproductive health care system and its delivery remains an important grey area due to certain distinctions inherent in them. Unmet health care need has a direct bearing on hard working capacity (Physical Labour) of a member in tribal society. Thereby quality of work suffers. (Sinha, et al 1980).

It has been noted that there is paucity of studies on many urgent issues affecting the health status of tribal women (National Commission for Women.1993).

The poor in the tribal areas cannot afford to spend on health from their family budgets and, therefore, are destined to suffer. An acceptable factor could be the indirect cost which is, many times the amount of direct medical expenses. The ratio (between) of the loss caused to the demoralized families due to traumatized experience associated with the health breakdown and, avoidance of overt expenditure, needs to be determined. Their primary earning hover around agriculture, fisheries, forestry, live stock, and allied activities. Poverty in agriculture sectors, at times, force tribals to take up jobs in non-farm activities. This distress diversification in their occupation makes their earning less remunerative. Therefore, the loss of productivity, which is beyond directly attributable cost of medical treatment, is not considered as a very important factor in Government policy formulation.

Children below 3 years of age in scheduled tribes are twice as likely to be malnourished than children in other groups. A person from the poorest quintile of the population, despite more health problems, is six times less likely to access hospitalization than a person from the richest quintile. This means that the poor are unable to afford and access hospitalization in a very large proportion of illness episodes, even when it is required. The delivery for a mother, from the poorest quintile of the population is over six times less likely to be attended by a medically trained person than the delivery by a well off mother, from the richest quintile of the population. (India Ministry of Tribal Affairs 2004).

Anam Ramanarayana Reddy, Minister (2007), A.P. Government observed at the second pre-annual conference, held in Nellore on 9-Dec-2007 that Producers in rural non farm sector are not able to get due price for their products because of the exploitative role played by middle men. This has significance because many of the Tribal families who have been forced off their forest homes have sought to cultivate degraded, infertile and often non-irrigated forest tracts on the outskirts of the forest. Tribals are also engaged in live stockbreeding.

There is a greater need for undertaking a region-specific study of the status and role of tribal women which alone can throw up data that will make planning for their welfare more meaningful and effective (.Singh. 1988).

The Health of Tribals is intertwined with the nature and eco system. The disturbance/ destruction in the forest eco- system has resulted in an urgent need for reviewing the health care system delivery. The bio-diversity pressures in the area include losing crop & livestock production, man-animal conflicts, timber & grazing, poaching and smuggling and of course, increasing tourism. A study among the Pauri

Bhuniyas of Orissa showed that 52 women as against 17 men in a sample of 268 persons suffered from diseases related to malnutrition. (Ali 1980).

In the present health care system there is some lacuna (there is a gap between the health care needs of the tribals and the care given by the governmental health care delivery agencies). It is an oft-felt need by all, which is reflected in electronic and print media often that the health care system for these Tribals, needs improvement.

"The sub optimal health status of indigenous peoples and the health inequalities between indigenous and non-indigenous populations reflect a fundamental failure to ensure the freedom of indigenous peoples to fully realize their human, social, economic, and political capabilities " (Sen 1999).

A number of studies on the social aspect of tribes, their culture and the impact of acculturation on the tribal society have been done. There have also been studies on the status of women relating to their socio- cultural problems, their economic rights, their rituals, their access to employment, food, etc. But these issues have not been properly focused in relation to the tribal Health care. The complications of pregnancy and of childbirth and of illegally induced abortions in areas where environmental and health conditions were adverse resulted in large numbers of tribal female deaths (United Nation Report 1984).

Although many in our country have given their opinion that privatization of the health care system can provide a meaningful solution, experience of other countries must discourage us with their unpleasant outcome. Morever in India tribal population is spread across different terrain and climatic conditions. Therefore, each area may need a different strategy for effective Health care delivery system.

Although United Nations observations go hand in hand on poor health of the tribal people with that of many Indian researchers, it would be apt to quote the National Health survey on key elements that disconnect in different stages the service delivery to be effective.

"Due to lapses at different points, the health care management system suffers a setback. There is a wide gap between the need and the supply. National Health Surveys provide adequate data on this topic" (National Health Survey).

Statement of the problem

There is a growing socio-economic inequality between rural and urban population. Basic inequality in health care benefits between rural and urban is increased by the rapid but unequal economic growth that India has witnessed in the last decade and half. Appalling poverty results in deprivation of even basic needs in general and health care in particular among the rural poor like tribal society.

Although a good number of researchers have put in efforts to identify the factors responsible for the difficulties in healthcare delivery in rural society, yet, one always feels that there are some dimensions, which are not explored. The fact that meeting health care need adequately is highly individualistic in nature which adds complexity to research work, but not conducting research work to identify the gaps will have ill-effect on the overall equilibrium in rural (Tribal) society and productivity besides the long term sustainability of the health care system in these areas.

A researcher needs to dig out and evaluate the influencing factors. Upon extraction of the information, crystallize and present it so that a long-term sustainable and effective health care delivery system can be formulated. This study evaluates the current healthcare model for tribals, and explores it in combination with the health status of the target population, placing emphasis on the long-term sustainability and cross-implementation of the health care delivery model.

Present study aims at analyzing various aspects of Health Care Services Delivery (HCSD) in tribal settlements, organizational setup and its operational management with a focus on conceptualizing operational problems by conducting field study of health care needs in selected tribal settlements.

Objectives of the study

1. To understand the perception of Tribal Society about the various dimensions of present health care system and its attitude to modern health care system.
2. To identify the problems faced by Tribals in seeking health care benefits.
3. To analyze the level of sensitivity of the health workers at ground level to the health needs of Tribals.
4. To determine how the organization climate is perceived by health care professionals to be optimally delivering the services and compare with the perception of the tribals.
5. To evaluate the health status of tribal school going children and explore the impact of education. .
6. To suggest the main approaches through which the problems of health care services delivery could be dealt with.

Research Hypotheses

The present study attempts to test the hypotheses that there is a poor heath care delivery in Tribal area. Tribals remain deprived of the benefits of health care from modern medical facilities. In spite of meticulous planning by government authorities some areas of health care needs are not covered due to the limitations of the system. A big achievement in health care will be to create a new system to address how the rural population in general and tribals in particular will be provided with overall health care coverage. Inequalities in health care between rural (Tribal) and urban areas have continued to increase. To ignore this problem is to invite problems in the future productivity and development of the country. This study tries to identify the factors responsible for the difficulties in healthcare delivery

Following hypotheses are set for the study-

1. Better health care infrastructure results in better health care services delivery
2. The perception of quality in health care services delivery are negatively associated among health care professionals and Tribals
3. There is an inadequate knowledge about the merits of modern health care system among tribals.
4. The lack of communication between health care professionals and tribals has resulted in ineffective delivery of the benefits of the health care system.

5. The sense of accomplishment or achievement is low among the health care professionals serving in tribal belt.
6. Schools going tribal children are deprived of health care coverage, which has adverse effect on their education.

Research Methodology

The study is based on primary data collected from Tribal settlements to seek the health care problems faced by tribals. Survey questionnaire is framed in a way that clearly elicits the required information like their awareness on health, need to visit qualified health care professionals, frustration with unmet health need, medicine etc. Survey method is adopted on the basis of simple random sampling. {Survey – Researcher read out the questionnaire explaining to them the details and purpose}.

In order to collect first hand information a direct personal interview was carried out. Interview method involved collection of data through direct verbal interaction between the interviewee and the interviewer (Sidhu 1989)

Observation method was adopted to assess the physical manifestation of illness among target groups. In the present study, both interview and observation methods course were adopted "where the budget and type of subject allow a combination of methods may provide a more valid estimate than any single method (Nicola et al .1986)

Pre-testing the Research Instrument

An informal testing of instrument was carried out with a small group of members of tribal society before finalizing the final draft of the instrument to confirm that they were universally held beliefs.

Osgood et al. conducted a classical research based on extensive factor analytic studies across culture. This study has shown that people understand, or give meaning to words or concepts along three dominant dimensions.

- The evaluative (Good-Bad) Dimension
- The Potency (Strong-Weak) Dimension
- Activity (Active-Passive) Dimension

This process involved two steps

a. Standardization - At the outset Instrument was examined by a panel of experts for expert comment in order to assess the ability of instrument to elicit the response from the respondents to meet the attributes sought in the research.
b. Reliability co-efficient of the Instrument- In order to ensure accurate response and to eliminate possible vacuum arising out of gap in communication, questionnaire was administered twice to the random sample of twenty-five respondents with the time- interval of about 20-25 days.

These respondents involved in pretesting were deleted from the mainstream of study. Pre-testing played a major role, as it was necessary to outline the perception of the respondents (Tribals) and to examine the meaningful outcome towards the requirement of the questionnaire. This process also ensured to capture adequate reflection of feelings, perceptions, experiences and delinquent behavior of the respondents.

Apart from the primary data, percentage, tabulation, ratios are used as a statistical devise to arrive at an inference. The data is collected from 535 samples. Simple random sampling was adopted for tribal universe of adults. A comprehensive schedule is used to collect data from target group covering tribal heads, members of the tribal families, Tribal primary school teachers and health care professionals around the settlements. Health care delivery system in tribal areas under study was examined from the perspective of the base hospital, by concentrating on mortality patterns, inpatient flow of selected infectious and non-infectious illnesses, the preventive and curative health services administered by the hospital to the community.

Design of the main study

The present study is descriptive in nature. The main theme of questionnaire was intended to measure the (a) perception, awareness and utility of health care services by tribal population (b) Intricacy, inconvenience and operational (on job) limitations of health care service delivery by health care professionals (c) First hand information, with regard to sickness of school going tribal children by school teachers.

Thus three group of respondents were chosen namely:

1. Respondents from adult tribal population
2. Health care professionals.
3. School Teachers of primary schools for tribals.

Total number of respondents were 535, spread across three above-mentioned groups. Upon deciding the variables, the sources and nature of the data were explored. This was done using the Chi-Square.

The data obtained was properly coded and analyzed with the help of a statistician using statistical package of social sciences (Nie et al.1975).

Frequency distribution of the two variables against each other was cross-tabulated. Frequency distribution of one variable is set out in columns and frequency distribution of the second variable was set out in rows. This enabled us to look at the distribution of one variable broken down within the different categories of another variable (Matt henn. et al 2006).

"Heuristics optimization routines" was adopted to shape the outcome of data analysis (Kotler 2004).

Limitations of the study

1. Respondent's memory had to be relied upon to collect data. At times, incoherence and inconsistency in the statement were observed.
2. Some respondents aggrieved by unsatisfactory emergency health care might have given an exaggerated version of the problems, which would have resulted in some bias in the statement.
3. The geographical area for the data collection was restricted to three districts.

REVIEW OF LITERATURE

It has been necessary to scan through the various work carried out in connection with the proposed study. This effort necessitated perusal of studies carried out by a range of luminaries whose work is connected directly or indirectly with the proposed work. This review is only a panoramic view of the entire spectrum of the studies done so far. The attempt here is to cull the findings of these outstanding luminaries. Different researchers' views have been taken into account to bring about a clarity and precision and to make the present work plausible and credible. In a way it is a journey backward to establish that the study is worth the research.

Tribals- a brief profile

The tribals are an ancient segment of population in India. India has the largest concentration of tribals next only to Africa in the world (Prerana Vaish 1988). By and large their living depends on agriculture and forest hunting so they earn just enough for their subsistence. Although there is special provision guaranteed by the constitution, health care facilities for the tribals need much improvement.

The Indian government identifies communities as scheduled tribes based on a community's "primitive traits, distinctive culture, shyness with the public at large, geographical isolation and social and economic backwardness" (India Ministry of Tribal Affairs 2004).

"While ''scheduled tribes'' is an administrative term adopted by the Government of India, the term ''Adivasis'' (meaning ''original inhabitants'' in Sanskrit) is often used to describe the different communities that belong to scheduled tribes. The Adivasis are thought to be the earliest settlers in, and the original inhabitants of, the Indian peninsula, with their presence dating back to before the Aryan colonization" (Thapar 1990).

Article 366 (25) of the Constitution of India refers to Scheduled Tribes as those communities who are scheduled in accordance with article 342 of the Constitution. This article states that only those communities who have been declared as such by the President through an initial public notification or through a subsequent amending act of Parliament will be considered to be Scheduled Tribes.

According to Article 342 of Indian Constitution the President of India notifies tribal communities. They are traditionally referred to as Tribes as they form minority ethnic groups with reference to their different languages customs, religious practices, economic backwardness, etc.

"Indigenous status in the context of India was operationalised through the Indian government's category of scheduled tribes, or Adivasis, which refers to people living in tribal communities characterized by distinctive social, cultural, historical, and geographical circumstances"(S. V. Subramanian1 et al).

"The concentration of scheduled tribes varies substantially between the Indian states" (Census ,2001).

Tribals have their share of contribution to enrich our cultural heritage by virtue of their distinctive identity (Naie, 1990).

The essential characteristics, first laid down by the Lokur Committee, for a community to be identified as Scheduled Tribes, are –

- Primitive traits;
- Distinctive culture;
- Shyness of contact with the community at large
- Geographical isolation
- Backwardness – social and economic.

A tribe is a collection of families bearing a common name, speaking a common dialect, occupying or professing to occupy a common territory (Chandrasekhar et al 1990).

They are often considered to be tribal people in the sense that they belong to small-scale pre-industrial societies that live in comparative isolation and manage their own affairs without the centralized authority of a state (Maybury-Lewis D 2002).

Tribal communities live in about 15% of the country's area, in various ecological and geo-climatic conditions ranging from plains and forests to hills and inaccessible areas. Tribal groups are at different stages of social, economic and educational development. Some tribal communities have adopted a mainstream way of life. At the other end of the spectrum, there are certain scheduled tribes (75 in number) known as Primitive Tribal Groups (PTGs), who are characterized by:

- A pre-agriculture level of technology;
- A stagnant or declining population;
- Extremely low literacy; and
- A subsistence level of economy.

(Ministry of Tribal Affairs 2006-07)

There are more than 400 tribal communities in our country. Among these, 74 tribal groups have been identified by the Government of India as Primitive (PTG) in 15 states and union territories (Neeti Mahanti 1991).

The following two maps show the spread of tribal population in Union Territories and the different states of India respectively.

Map 2.1-TRIBAL POPULATION IN UNION TERRITORIES

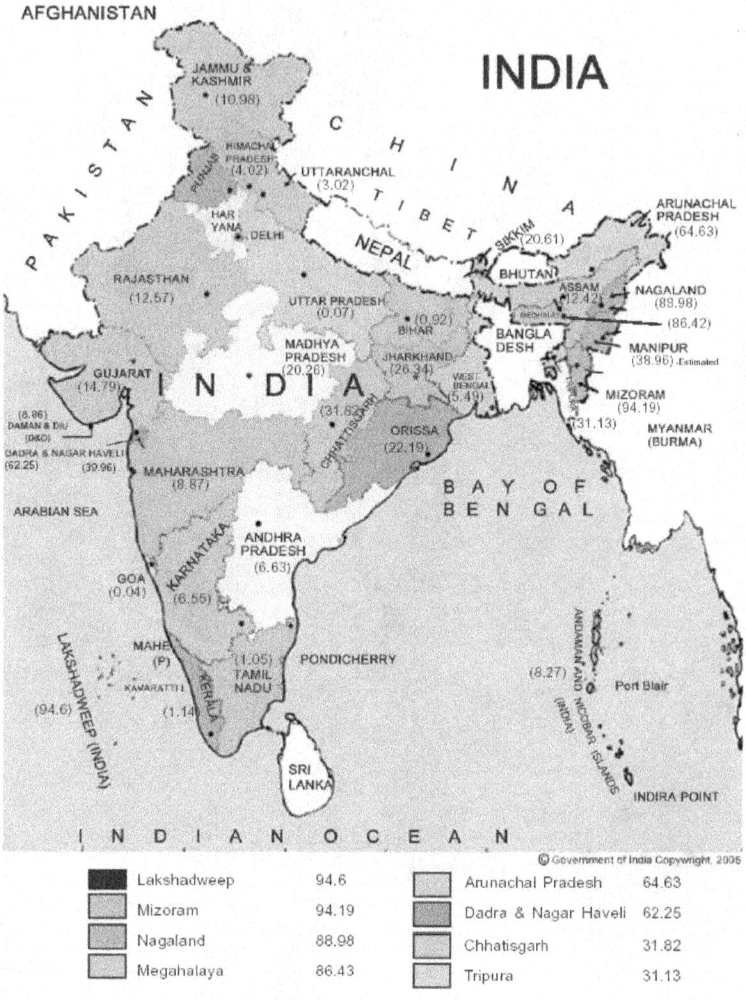

Map-2.2TRIBAL POPULATION IN DIFFERENT STATES OF INDIA

Table 2.1 -Distribution Of Tribal Population Across The Country

No.	State / U.T.	Total	Males	Females
1	India	84,326,240	42,640,829	41,685,411
2	Andaman & Nicobar Islands	29,469	15,127	14,342
2	Andaman & Nicobar Islands	29,469	15,127	14,342
3	Andhra Pradesh	5,024,104	2,548,295	2,475,809
4	Arunachal Pradesh	705,158	352,017	353,141
5	Assam	3,308,570	1,678,117	1,630,453
6	Bihar	758,351	393,114	365,237
7	Chandigarh	NN	NN	NN
8	Chhattisgarh	6,616,596	3,287,334	3,329,262
9	Dadra & Nagar Haveli	137,225	67,663	69,562
10	Daman & Diu	13,997	7,190	6,807
11	Delhi	NN	NN	NN
12	Goa	566	299	267
13	Gujarat	7,481,160	3,790,117	3,691,043
14	Haryana	NN	NN	NN
15	Himachal Pradesh	244,587	122,549	122,038
16	Jammu & Kashmir	1,105,979	578,949	527,030
17	Jharkhand	7,087,068	3,565,960	3,521,108
18	Karnataka	3,463,986	1,756,238	1,707,748
19	Kerala	364,189	180,169	184,020
20	Lakshadweep	57,321	28,611	28,710
21	Madhya Pradesh	12,233,474	6,195,240	6,038,234
22	Maharashtra	8,577,276	4,347,754	4,229,522
23	Manipur	741,141	374,319	366,822
24	Meghalaya	1,992,862	996,567	996,295
25	Mizoram	839,310	422,963	416,347
26	Nagaland	1,774,026	913,203	860,823
27	Orissa	8,145,081	4,066,783	4,078,298
28	Pondicherry	NN	NN	NN
29	Punjab	NN	NN	NN
30	Rajasthan	7,097,706	3,650,982	3,446,724
31	Sikkim	111,405	56,940	54,465
32	Tamil Nadu	651,321	328,917	322,404
33	Tripura	993,426	504,320	489,106
34	Uttar Pradesh	107,963	55,834	52,129
35	Uttaranchal	256,129	131,334	NN
36	West Bengal	4,406,794	2,223,924	2,182,870

Source: Census of India 2001
Notes: - NN not notified

However, the Government of India has resisted the use of the term "indigenous" when referring to the scheduled tribes on the grounds that is a practical impossibility to decide indigenousness after centuries of migration, absorption, and differentiation as reflected in 'the National Policy on Tribals' draft. A formal recognition of the indigenousness of the scheduled tribes is also interpreted as contradictory to the overall spirit underlying the recognition of the tribal populations, which is to facilitate ''assimilation'' of the tribal population into the country's mainstream. Indigenous populations are similar to those seen within the non-indigenous population" (The National Tribal Policy 2004).

Studies on Tribal Health and Health Care Delivery

Enormous wealth of literature on tribal health is available but it is impossible to trawl through everything. Although there are numerous studies done both at national and regional level, a close look suggests that there are hardly any studies done on health care management and its delivery in tribal areas.

In order to make the study more systematic, a number of articles and studies were considered to review the Health Care Services Delivery in tribal areas. It is a fact and a matter of concern that, even after six decades following the independence of our country, the tribals are deprived of basic health care benefits. Since the study deals with inadequate health care system and poor management of its delivery in tribal areas, works, observation and research works from important studies both at national and international level have been considered. In the present study an attempt has been made to review the available literature on health among tribal population to indicate their existing health status and to identify the gaps to suggest a practical plan of action besides pointing out the debatable issues.

The Ministry of Tribal Affairs is the nodal ministry for the overall policy, planning and coordination of programmes for the development of Scheduled Tribes. The programmes and schemes of the ministry are intended to support and supplement, through financial assistance, the efforts of other central ministries, the state governments and voluntary organizations, and to fill critical gaps taking into account the present situation of the tribals. Though the primary responsibility for the promotion of interests of Scheduled Tribes rests with all the Central Ministries, the

Ministry of Tribal Affairs complements their efforts by way of various developmental interventions in critical sectors through specially tailored schemes (Ministry of Tribal Affairs Annual Report 2007).

Dr. Ganesh. N. Devy, the founder trustee of Bhasha Research and Publication Center in Baroda, wrote in the periodical dated 23 May 2005, "The earliest expression of their (tribal) agony could be traced in the report of a reform committee headed by Antrolikar on the eve of India's independence. But the issue had to wait till early eighties. Number matters in democracies even for a small measure to be effective and mainly because with a weak fabric of social justice holding it together."

The Tribal Sub Plan strategy was developed by an Expert Committee set up by the Ministry of Education and Social Welfare in 1972 under the Chairmanship of Prof. S. C. Dube for the rapid socio-economic development of tribal people and was adopted for the first time in the Fifth Five Year Plan (Fifth Five Year Plan, GOI).

"There are other organizations like NGOs, charitable trusts, etc. which provide health care services. Tribal populations generally have poor health outcomes, often because of a healthcare delivery system that does not cater to their needs" (National Medicine Journal of India, 2005).

Illiteracy and poverty have led to ignorance of benefits of modern medical findings among the tribals. This is borne out by the fact that "more than 90 percent of the deliveries were conducted at home attended by elderly ladies of the household. No specific precautions were observed at the time of conducting deliveries, which resulted in an increased susceptibility to various infections. Services of paramedical staff were secured only in difficult labour cases" (National Commission for Women, New Delhi 93).

A study by Kuriyan et al. (1982) showed that understaffing of primary healthcare centres is the main cause for the tribals to be deprived of the health care benefits.

A retrospective observational study from the year 2000, aimed at current healthcare delivery model offered to a Malayali and Lambadi tribal population in Dharmapuri district, concluded that the base tribal hospital is important in administering primary and secondary health care and health education for continuous confidence in allopathic medicine. This study was necessisitated in the light of the inadequate health infrastructure for the tribal population in Dharmapuri district (Hari Prabhakar et al. 2005 b)

"Most of the tribal population is desperately poor, backward, generally uneducated and lead a very hard and miserable life" (Thakur et al. 1991).

A study on tribals in different parts of the country by the Ministry of Tribal Affairs (2007a) suggests that there is no adequate reach of health care services in tribal areas. "The infant mortality, under-5 child mortality and percentage of children under-weight in respect of Tribes are higher than that of the overall population as well as of other disadvantaged socio economic groups."

Das et al. (2000) on the viability of a tribal health programme in Gujarat, cited understaffing of primary healthcare centres, exploitation of migrant laborers, and inadequate supplies of medicines as primary causes of underdevelopment and poor health outcomes. The widespread poverty, illiteracy, malnutrition, absence of safe drinking water and sanitary living conditions, poor maternal and child health services and ineffective coverage of national health and nutritional services have been identified in several studies as possible contributing factors to dismal health conditions prevailing among the tribal population in India. In this article, the author focuses on certain factors like infant mortality rate, life expectancy, genetic disorders, sexually transmitted diseases, nutritional status, forest ecology, child health and health care practices which are generally responsible for determining the health status and health behaviour of tribal communities (Dimensions of Tribal Health 2000).

The tribals originally depended on their native herbal medicines for cure of their illnesses. Availing the modern health care system itself is a new life style for them. It is an accepted fact in India that for some diseases like jaundice even an urbanite resorts to herbal cure. Therefore it is not surprising that tribals have evolved some successful cures out of their own ecosystem / biosphere. Use of herbal medicine in their day-to-day life is an inherent part of the tribal life.

A survey on delivery of health care services in poor areas suggested that public health care services for the poor often involve a lot of non-financial costs such as waiting time, lack of access and inadequate facilities such as hospital beds, equipment and medicines (Economic Survey 2006-2007).

Dr M.B.Bhiradi and S.C.Biradar (2002) pointed out that 103 taluks in Karnataka needed 11 types of basic infrastructure development.

"The ratio of hospital beds to population in rural areas is fifteen times lower than that for urban areas. The ratio of doctors to population in rural areas is almost six times lower than that in the urban population" (Central Bureau of Health Intelligence 2001).

According to the Ministry of Tribal Affairs (2007b), lack of data is a constraint when it comes to tracking the health indicators of the tribal population. Data on health does not contain information disaggregated by social groups on a regular basis.

A report on human development in Karnataka which was published in Status of Scheduled Tribes in Karnataka 2005, indicate that the degree of effectiveness in terms of programme implementation is poor and is evident in the three critical areas of health, education and poverty reduction. The magnitude of the problem is so great that a large percentage of Scheduled Tribes families is still poor and lacks access to resources that would improve their education and health status. Human development status of the Scheduled Tribes is more than a decade behind than that of the rest of the population of the state and they are the poorest and the most deprived of all sub-populations in the state (Tribes in Karnataka 2005).

Inability to reach health care center for medical services due to distance and inadequate infrastructure have led to poor delivery of health care benefits for tribals. A study among a tribal population of Gujarat cited the major breakdown in active surveillance, coupled with the inaccessibility of health agencies near affected villages as the cause of the outbreak of malaria (Srivastava et al. 2003).

There are many studies related to the high prevalence of diseases among tribals. While conducting a morbidity study among the Kondha tribe of Phulbani district, Orissa, Swain (1990) found syphilis (10 percent) in Desia Kondhs, whereas it was not diagnosed among the primitive Kutia Kondh tribal group. The presence of sexually transmitted diseases was also reported from Andamanese, tribal groups of Madhya Pradesh, Rajasthan, Mysore, etc. (Swain et al 1990)

A study has shown that over 55 percent of Kondhs consumed food providing less than 2000 calories per day and most of them as little as 1700 calories, compared to the ICMR (Indian Council Medical Council) stipulated requirement of 2400 calories (Patel, 1985).

A survey conducted by the Ministry of Tribal Affairs (2007c) reveals that the health status of the tribal population is not on par with the rest of the state's population. Most of the health indicators show deterioration in the health of women and children.

There exists a definite relation between forests and nutrition of Tribals. It has been noted by many that tribals living in remote areas have a better overall status and eat a more balanced diet than tribals living in less remote, forest free areas. The mode of utilization of available natural resources often determines the long-term impact on health (Basu, 1993).

Inadequate data on tribal health care has led to improper planning. The health status is the outcome of a combination of both infrastructure and delivery of health care services.

David et al (2001) observed that India needs to set its sights on developing a more efficient and equitable health financing system. This means a financing system that has compulsory membership, a socially acceptable and affordable package of benefits, pre-payment, and risk pooling for people with different incomes and health status. The main questions are when and how to get there.

A study on healthcare delivery in Sittilingi tribal area showed that, taking into consideration the ability of an allopathic healthcare delivery system to provide health services to a relatively small tribal population, a bias does arise when using hospital-based data to reflect the health status of the tribal population in general, given that persons who avail of hospital services are (i) those individuals who are sick, and (ii) those who have confidence in allopathic interventions (Hari Prabhakar et al . 2005).

In the absence of statistical information on the qualitative aspect of health care provision, quantitative indicators of available health facilities are likely to provide imprecise measures of the services actually supplied. Also the relationship between health care provision and child mortality may be hard to identify.

A good example would be of the Onges. If tribals are not given good health coverage it would be disastrous. For example, the Onges, who once occupied the whole island of Little Andaman, were reduced to a mere handful. Their population is declining fast and they are on the verge of extinction. The problems faced by the Onges are similar to that of the Andamanese. Their habitat, which once occupied the whole island, has been reduced to two small settlements. There is a primary health centre at Dugong Creek exclusively for the Onges, whose population is a little over one hundred (ICMR).

The Centre has carried out some studies on the health and nutritional problems and the demography of the Onge population. The population of the Onges over the last 100 years is shown below. It is observed that there has been a precipitous fall in their population strength from 1901 to 1950 followed by a gradual decrease in their number until 1990. This decline was attributed to wars, epidemic diseases, high mortality exceeding that of fertility and incompatible pairing of marriage partners leading to unproductive marriages. There is now a marginal increase in their number to 105.

Diagram - 2.1 : Change in the population of Onges in 20th Century

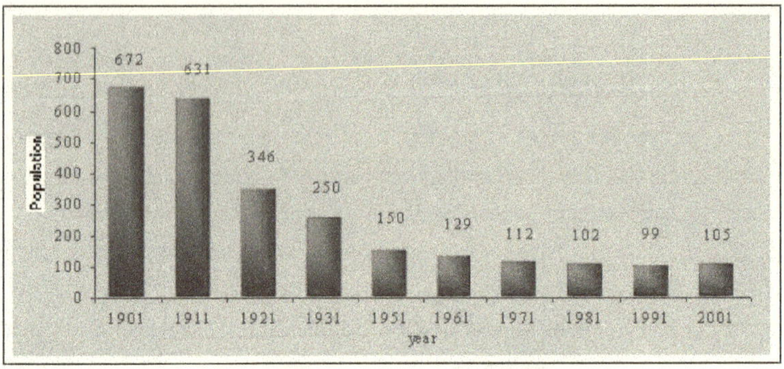

Haemoglobin estimation was done in 67 Onges and 58 (86.6%) of them were found to be anemic. Twenty-one of the 109 babies born alive to the 27 married women in the community died before completing their first year of life, giving an overall Infant Mortality Rate of 192.7 per 1000 live births during the past 30 years. This is much higher than the IMR in rural India, which declined from 136 in 1970 to 105 in 1985 and again to 79 in 1994. 30 children among the 109 live-born babies died before attaining 5 years of age and 12 more died after the age of 5 years giving a total of 63 childhood deaths. The total child mortality rate is 578 per 1000 live births. Only 58 of the 109 live born babies survived up to the age of five years giving an under-five mortality rate of 468/1000 live births and a child survival rate of only 53.2%.

There are a number of studies done to understand the perception of the poor about quality health care services. Physical access to health care center, affordability of treatment and effective treatment are the parameters set by the poor. But their ability to seek care depends on their awareness about health problem. Familiarity with service providers often put them at ease and they are eager to go to those centers they are familiar with.

A study conducted by Dr. Nirmala Murthy (2006) based on data from four districts of Karnataka and Rajasthan had interesting observations. In this study the researcher interviewed about 900 poor and non-poor women who had experienced various reproductive health problems. The main objective of the study was to find out differences in their experiences in the quality of care they received and the treatment effectiveness of the treatment. It was observed that poor women preferred government services for pre-natal care and family planning not because those services were free but because these women felt the services were good. The researcher supposed that the reason was that the government workers had targets to fulfill and therefore they treated women with respect because they were helping to fulfill the targets set by the government.

On the other hand, for childbirth, women preferred homes. That is not only because homes were a convenient location but also because many women feared that they would be forced to undergo un-necessary caesarean operation at hospitals to extract money from them. Poor women often expressed doubts about the quality of medicines they received or the doctor's diagnosis.

This study clearly brings out the fact that good incentives in rural areas can bring about quality service delivery in the health care sector. Yet another factor is the impression that the rural poor have about the business-like attitude of the health care professionals. Their past experience has led to their belief that there is overcommercialisation of health care services.

In a similar study by Basu(1993), it was found that the main causes of maternal mortality were found to be unhygienic and primitive practices for parturition. For example, it was observed that among the Kutia Kondhs tribals, the delivery was conducted by the mother herself in a half squatting position holding a rope hanging down from the roof of the hut. This helped her in applying pressure to deliver the child. In complicated labour, this often led to maternal as well as child mortality.

Taneja et al. (1997) conducted a survey among the Bhil tribe of Jhabua district and observed that lack of health care facility was a major cause of death among neonates. Some of these deaths which were preventable were due to tetanus, diarrhoea, measles, acute respiratory infections and fever.

In a nutritional and demographic study (Prema et al. 1992) of Kannikar tribal women of Trivandrum district, Kerala, normal and physiological conditions like pregnancy and lactation were studied. Important sources of protein like pulses, milk and milk products and other animal foods were lacking in their diets. Average calorie consumption was found to be below the recommended level for normal, pregnant as well as lactating women. Detailed clinical examination of the Kannikar tribal women showed that anaemia (90 percent), vitamin A deficiency (30 percent) and niacin deficiency (10 percent) were prevalent among them. The morbidity status of the tribal women revealed the prevalence of pyrexia, respiratory complaints, gastro-intestinal diseases and rheumatic diseases. Among the adult women gynecological complaints and deficiency diseases were common (Basu, 1993).

Shah (1989) conducted a study on quality of health services in rural India and observed, "The availability of health care services can reasonably be expected to have a negative impact on child mortality; however, it should be remembered that the functioning of health services can be as important as their availability. Many studies have demonstrated the poor functioning of health services in large parts of the rural India."

Sukhatme (1993), Padma Bhushan, stressed on the restructure on health care delivery system. In his supplementary note on a report of The Expert Group on Estimation of Proportion and Number of Poor he wrote, "Actual examination of stools confirm that one out of every two episodes is bacterial in origin, thereby pointing to the annual prevalence of diarrhoea of the order of 40 to 50%. The high mortality that we find in children is in fact the result of this high prevalence of morbidity. A child with infection will not grow. It is not therefore so much the intake that determines work capacity; it is the control of disease that matters. I fear that continuing food intervention under these conditions will be to waste our resources. Clearly our programme needs to be restructured and that too very soon."

According to Singh et al (2001), tribal areas are inaccessible. High immunization rates among tribal children may be achieved through targeting illiterate mothers in inaccessible areas. These first-contact primary interventions, in turn, may also lessen the increasing rates of youth mortality seen among tribals.

Basu et al. (1993) while conducting research investigation on 481 households among the Jaunsaris of Jaunsar Bawar, Dehradum, found a crude birth rate of 42.67 per thousand and infant mortality rate of 79.64 per thousand live births.

Studies of tribal communities in Orissa conducted by Ali (1992) found that an ecological imbalance caused by rapid deforestation had resulted not only in depleting food resources, but also in prolonged droughts, adding to hunger and starvation.

Chang et al (2003) opined that for the poor, apart from the financial burden, there were the effects of ill health too. If left untreated or partially treated, the disease in question would get aggravated resulting in death or disability. On the other hand, self-medication, which was often practiced, resulted in incorrect self-diagnosis and inappropriate dosage, thereby inducing side effects.

Most of the tribal population is deprived of the benefits of modern health care system. A study done on health care among Kunabi Tribe of Karnataka revealed that traditional healers are present in certain villages and over 45 species of plants are still used in the area to treat a wide range of ailments such as fever, cough, skin diseases, rheumatism, snake-bite, jaundice and dysentery (Hebbar et al. 2002).

Maternal and child health care practices were found to be largely neglected in various tribal groups, namely, Baster tribal groups, Kutia Kondhs of Orissa, Santals, Jaunsaris, Kharias, etc. Expectant mothers to a large extent were not inoculated against tetanus. From the inception of pregnancy to its termination, women consumed no specific nutritious diet. On the other hand, some pregnant tribal women (i.e. Dudh Kharias, Santals) reduced their food intake because of the fear of recurrent vomiting and also to ensure that the baby remains small, so that the delivery may be easier. The consumption of iron, calcium and vitamins during pregnancy was poor. The habit of taking alcohol during pregnancy was found to be common among the tribal women and almost all of them continued their regular activities, including hard labour, even during advanced pregnancy. More than 90 percent of the deliveries were conducted at home attended by elderly ladies of the household. No specific precautions were observed at the time of conducting deliveries, which resulted in increased mortality.

The nutritional problems of different tribal communities located at various stages of development were full of obscurities and very little scientific information on dietary habits and nutrition status was available due to lack of systematic and comprehensive research investigations. Malnutrition was common and greatly affected the ability to resist infection, which led to chronic illnesses and, in the post-weaning period, to permanent brain impairment (National Commission for Women 1993).

Indigenous-nonindigenous health divide is a reflection of the differences in socio-economic well being between indigenous and non-indigenous groups. If unequal distribution of socio-economic resources accounts for indigenous-nonindigenous health inequalities, there is an urgent need to redress the pervasive and chronic socio-economic inequalities.

Tribal people have always lived in forests. They lived on forest produce and used agriculture for their subsistence. Today the modern world has encroached into the tribal life, causing insecurity, confusion and ill health.

"Indigenous groups experience excess mortality compared to non-indigenous groups." (Subramanian 2006).

Many of the tribal societies (Vidyarthi et al.1977) were lax towards pre-marital sex relations, which were considered as training in the art of love and sex life and often ended in marriage.

The widespread poverty, illiteracy, malnutrition, absence of safe drinking water and sanitary living conditions, poor maternal and child health services and ineffective coverage of national health and nutritional services have been found in several studies as possible contributing factors to dismal health conditions prevailing among the tribal population in India (Dimension Of tribal health 2000).

The environment plays a critical role in the framework and evaluation of a health system. A study in Sittilingi tribal area showed that the geographical area and the socioeconomic status of the tribals deprived them of modern health care benefits. The rough and hilly terrain of Sittilingi could only be traversed via jeep, bus or motorcycle (Hari Prabhakar et al. 2005a).

Even though there is a high fertility rate among the tribals, lack of medical facility have led to high mortality of newborn babies. Murty and Ramesh (1978) found a high fertility and mortality among the Pardhans of Adilabad district (BMJ 1992).

The study of Sirajuddin et al (1984) among the Chenchu tribal group of Achampet taluk of Andhra Pradesh found that the average number of children for each woman, the average number of surviving offspring per married woman and mortality in relation to live births were 3.67 %, 2.96 % and 27.5 % respectively.

An epidemiological survey of tribal villages in southern Bihar revealed that there is no health care facility in tribal areas and noted that a lack of health awareness in the area remained the primary obstacle towards improved community health (Friedman et al. 2002).

A study on tribal women suggests that health of tribal women cannot be ignored. It becomes important because the problems of tribal women differ from one particular area to another, owing to their geographical location, historical background and the processes of social change (Chauhan et al. 1990).

Basu (1967) conducted a demographic research work among the Irular tribals of Tamil Nadu and reported the net reproductive index, which was also an indication of their fertility, as 1.31. It was also reported that mortality according to the age of the child was highest in the first year (BMJ 1992).

While evaluating the impact of the family welfare programme on tribal women through a study of 300 tribal women of Tamian development block of Chindwara district of Madhya Pradesh, it was observed that tribal women gave more attention to child welfare and child development programmes rather than to mother care or family planning programmes (Tekhre 1989).

Pandey [1990] observed high fertility and mortality in Mishmi tribal groups and attributed it to the low level of education and income, lack of knowledge of family planning methods and the importance of small family size, poor medical facilities and lack of proper sanitation and drinking water.

Due to illiteracy, tribals form their own opinion about diseases and remain away from modern line of treatment. Despite the availability of modern facilities of treatment, Tharus (Tribals in Naintal) had their own beliefs and concepts of disease (Kumar et al. 1975).

According to Godwin et al (2005), since there is a negative relationship between self-medication and household economic status, the poor resort more to self-medication. Drug forms a very important component of it. Hence rising prices may affect the poor the most.

Mishra et al. (2003) conducted a study to assess the benefits from development of newer drugs for poor. It was revealed that the profit maximizing companies mostly concentrated on the development of drugs that treated the diseases of the rich. For example, of the 1700 odd drugs developed between 1975 and 1998 in the world, only 13 drugs were developed for the poor man's tropical diseases.

Murty (1987) investigated the Soliga tribe in Karnataka in order to find out their fertility behaviour. The Crude Birth Rate (CBR), General Fertility Rate (GFR) and Total Fertility Rate (TFR) among the Soligas were found to be always higher in comparison to the general population of Karnataka. The unusual high fertility rate among the Soligas was influenced by their age at marriage, which was ultimately influenced by the age at menarche. The mean age of menarche among the Soligas was 13.2 years and the age of marriage was 14.2 years, which was very early. Early age of marriage and low levels of family planning acceptance seemed to be responsible for the high fertility among the Soligas. The completed family size among the Soligas was 5.64 (Status of Tribal Women in India 1993).

Aggarwal (1967) found that among 45 married Onge women of the Andaman Islands, the mean number of children was 1.64 and the mean number of children per women was 1.13. Infant mortality was very high as revealed from the reproductive index, which was 0.51 (Status of Tribal Women in India 1993).

Good health and good society go together. This is possible only when supportive services such as nutrition, environment and education reach a higher level. Maternal and childcare is an important aspect of health seeking behavior, which is largely neglected among the tribal groups (Basu et al., 1990).

Chaudhuri, (1990) conducted studies across many tribal groups to get an understanding of their health care management and found that they use different parts of a plant not only for the treatment of diseases, but for population control as well. Medical expenses are very high if treatment is received in private health clinics. Poor cannot afford the expenses.

Devadasan (2004) examined the exorbitant medical expenses incurred by the poor. "It is estimated that at least 24% of all out-of-pocket spending on hospital care might have been raised by 2% of the proportion of the population in poverty."

The study of demographic and health determinants of infant deaths by Gurumurthy et al. (1990) among the Sugali tribal group in the Kalyanadurga and Beluguppa blocks of Ananthapur district of Andhra Pradesh pointed out that out of 348 infant deaths 45.4 percent were neonatal and 54.6 per cent were post neonatal. About 25 percent infant deaths occurred due to dysentery / diarrhea and 20 percent due to maternal factors such as prematurity, birth injury, multiple birth, low birth weight, birth asphyxia and so on (NFHS-II India1998-99).

The sickle cell disease was found in 72 districts of Central, Western and Southern India. There were more than 35 tribal population groups showing a frequency of more than 19 percent. It was estimated that approximately a staggering 50 lakh individuals were carriers (heterozygotes) among the tribals (Basu et al. 1990).

Prevalence rate up to 40 percent of heterozygous form (sickle cell trait) was reported in some tribes i.e. Adiyan of Kerala, Irula, Paniyan, Mulukurumbha of Nilgiri hills and Gonds of Rajpur (Basu, 1993).

(Sickle cell disease is a genetic disorder characterizing a shortened life span of the red cell leading to severe and often fatal anemia (Reduced Red Blood Cells). The disease is further characterized by enlarged spleen, organ damage, impaired mental functions and increased susceptibility to infection).

Poverty has a great role to play in deprivation of health care benefit. "A child in the 'Low Standard of Living' economic group is almost four times more likely to die in childhood than a child in the 'High Standard of Living' group. Child born in the tribal belt is one and half times more likely to die before the fifth birthday than children of other groups. Female child is 1.5 times more likely to die before reaching her fifth birthday as compared to a male child" (NFHS-II, India1998-99.)

A large number of poor are deprived of protein and essential vitamins in their food, which is an essential promoter of body defense to fight infection. Poor nutrition could retard the growth of children and cause anemia in tribal women.

According to a United Nations report, good nutrition was a requirement throughout life and was vital to women in terms of their health and work. Nutritional anemia was a major problem for women in India and more so in the rural and tribal belt. In developing countries, it was estimated that at least half of the non-pregnant and two thirds of the pregnant women were anemic (United Nations Report 1984).

Studies carried out at the National Institute of Nutrition (1971) and Planning Commission of India (Sixth Five Year Plan, Government of India) on the diets of South Indian tribes reported high protein calorie malnutrition along the rice-eating belts. Therefore alleviation of poverty is a cornerstone through employment in rural belts, which alone can improve nutritional status of the tribals. Government should allocate resources towards this.

Malnutrition was common and greatly affected the ability to resist infection, leading to chronic illness and, in the post-weaning period, to permanent brain impairment. The outcome indicators of health (mortality, morbidity and life expectancy) are all directly influenced by the standards of living of a given population. Moreover, it is not the absolute deprivation of income that matters, but the relative distribution of income (Wilkinson 1992).

Poor and inadequate health care for tribals is a concern in many parts of the world. According to the International Institute for Population Sciences, a tribal female child is 1.5 times more likely to die before reaching her fifth birthday as compared to a male child. "A tribal mother is over 12 times less likely to be delivered by a medically trained person. A tribal woman is one and a half times more likely to suffer the consequences of chronic malnutrition as compared to women from other social categories" (NFHS-II India1998-99).

Privatization process does undoubtedly bring a divide between "the Haves" and "the Have-nots". The poor will again suffer a disadvantage. "There is an undisputed association between social equality, social integration and health. The effect of social integration on health is conclusively documented in the theory of 'social support'" (Cassel.J, 1976).

Colonization in some parts of the world had lured the indigenous population into consumption of alcohol and excess usage of tobacco. At times, indigenous youth considered this usage as a symbol of prestige and so that, in using them, they would be considered as belonging to the "evolved modern generation" in society. There are a good number of studies on this subject.

"The excess use of tobacco and alcohol among indigenous groups observed in this study is important in its own right as well as in terms of its contribution to accounting for the excess mortality, though in this study we were unable to examine the latter directly since information on tobacco and alcohol consumption was not ascertained for the deceased household members. The excess use of tobacco and alcohol in some indigenous populations has been shown to be linked to the process of colonization and increased aping of Western culture" (Seale JP et al 2002).

Good nutrition is a requirement throughout life for human body and is vital especially to a pregnant woman. Poor nutrition due to poverty (and sometimes due to cultural taboos) resulted in ill health. "Tribal population suffers a great degree of deprivation due to cultural beliefs, prejudices, taboos and superstitions" (U.N.Report 1984).

Impact of Unique Health Care Initiatives for Tribals

Julie Louise Gerberding, Director, Centers for Disease Control and Prevention, US, in an interview with "Scientific American" in January 2007 said, "We have to pick our highest priorities and concentrate on things we can do in a cost effective manner to make the biggest impact. I believe it is much more economical to prevent problems than wait to treat the disease they cause."

There are a few well-designed health care programmes implemented for tribals in our country. This has brought immense relief to a few tribal settlements. These efforts and impacts are creditable by all standards. Each of these progammes is different from the other, and its impact on the health of the population is remarkable. Following are a few important examples.

In the poorest village of central India (Dhar District,Madhya Pradesh), the villagers and the district collector have provided an innovative health service, with the barest of resources. The concept of a 'community delivery room' is an attempt by Dhar District Collector (DC) Rajesh Rajoura to tackle the district's very high maternal and child mortality rates. The Community Delivery Room (CDR) scheme was set up in May 1999 following a demand from the village panchayats (elected councils), set up under India's legal directive, to divert power to villages for self-help. With Primary Health Centres (PHCs) few and far between, unhygienically conducted home deliveries resulted in complications. With the CDR initiative came the first signs of change. The panchayats offered space in panchayat buildings and anganwadi (child-welfare) centres to the DC in exchange for training local midwives. The DC, in turn, took the government's Integrated Tribal Development Programme (ITDP) funds for infrastructural equipment like furniture and utensils, setting aside an annual amount for medicines.

The midwife then managed the CDR with the nurse (ANM), while the sarpanch (elected village headman) assumed responsibility for maintenance and recurring expenses. United Nations International Children's Fund (UNICEF) supports midwife training. Although 54 CDRs were begun experimentally, all turned out to be successful. CDRs assume reproductive and child health (RCH) duties. This programme would be popularised in other districts in time. (Mr. Rajesh Rajoura District Collector, Dhar District,Madhya Pradesh, India Madhya Pradesh Govt Website).

A similar example is from B R Hills tribal project initiated by Dr Sudarshan in Chamrajnagar district of Karnataka, South India. Inspired by Mahatma Gandhi, Dr. Regi and Dr. Lalitha started a pilot scheme in Bailhongal Taluka, Belgaum District, with just a thatched hut for outpatient consulting in 1993 (Mani Kalliath 2001).

A similar effort was put forth by the government of Orissa, realizing that basic education is indispensable for the improvement in overall development and health of the tribal society (tribal.nic.in website).

The construction of the Eklavya Model Residential School, Dhanghera, under Khunta Block, Mayurbhanj, Orissa, turned out to be a success. The project "Construction of the Eklavya Model Residential School, Dhanghera" was taken up with the intention of providing better education infrastructure to the tribal students of the area. The project was sanctioned out of Special Grant and the construction work commenced on 26-11-2001. It took exactly two years to complete and Shri Nabin Pattanaik, Hon'ble Chief Minister, Orissa, inaugurated the building on 2nd March 2006. Since then the school has been functioning with 367 inmates, providing better education and hostel facilities.

The "Tribal India Health Foundation" is a non-profit organization formed out of the existing tribal health initiatives to significantly improve the health status of their target populations, while also encouraging the formation of more tribal health initiatives throughout India. This will enable tribal populations to break their current cycle of poverty and ill health and to enjoy better lives.

The Tribal India Health Foundation, with its partners, also supports the Sickle-Cell Disease Treatment and Research Center in South India to alleviate the burden of sickle-cell disease among the resident tribal and non-tribal populations of the area. Partner organizations offer a 4-week Public Health and Preventive Medicine elective program for medical and public health students in the US.

The Tribal India Health Foundation has the following program objectives:

- Strengthening the capacity of organizations dedicated to tribal health to identify and address the health needs of the communities in which they work
- Spreading the benefits of the foundation to new partners and their respective beneficiaries
- Promoting additional interest, support, research, and funding for tribal health initiatives in the private sector

The other partner organizations and individuals include:

- The East West Foundation of India (www.tewfi.org)
- Give Hand (www.giveahand.org)
- The Health and Human Rights Group at Johns Hopkins School of Public Health (www.jhspf.edu)

A pertinent example is the tribal village in Sittilingi. Before 1993 no local doctors lived in Sittilingi, a remote tribal village in Dharmapuri district of Tamil Nadu. The nearest hospital was 50 kilometers away. Death rate of children and adults was high due to malnutrition, diarrhea, dehydration, etc. All this was to change when Dr. Regi and Dr. Lalitha started Tribal Health Initiative in 1993 with just a thatched hut for outpatient consulting.

Now the Tribal Hospital can accommodate 24 in-patients. The hospital offers emergency and ambulance facilities. The children of Sittilingi no longer face an uncertain world due to lack of knowledge and inadequate medical facilities. Sittilingi is now also supported by a number of tribal women trained as health auxiliaries by Tribal Health Initiative programmes.

Two new initiatives have recently been taken up as part of the holistic approach to Tribal Development in the area: Tribal Education Initiative and Tribal Farm Initiative

Dr. Mani Kalliath (2006), an external evaluator, had the following observations to make based on the 10 years evaluation of the Tribal Health Initiative in Sittilingi. The "Impact Evaluation" programme of Tribal Health Initiative brought out immense strengths of the organisation in its health care interventions. High quality service is provided through its community-based cadres in raising health awareness, changing superstitious practices and in promoting health-seeking behaviours. By all standards these outcomes and impacts are creditable and the organisation is a credible resource, in the poor tribal setting who are deprived of resources.

The health systems of many high-income countries like Japan and China have undergone reforms in the past few decades. The main motivation for such reforms has often been health related productivity, and the main challenge has been to control costs while maintaining or broadening access to high-quality care for all members of society. Such studies may be of interest in dealing with tribal healthcare in the Indian context.

A meaningful insight can be drawn from China's rural health care system. It is significant to note that the system looks at the changes in the individual's health care situation between the present and preceding 10 years to determine if there has been any significant change within that time period.

"It is hypothesized that market reform continues and thus does health care reform. But privatization leads to more inequity in health care distribution because of the non-uniform health care policies ". (Brian A. Wong et al. 1986).

Thomas Smith (1959) in the "Agrarian Origins of Modern Japan'' outlines many of the rural developments in the Tokugawa period that ultimately led to the modern state of Japan.

Continuous up gradation of existing data is an important step to pinpoint the healthcare need of tribals. But in a developing country like India there are very few systematic, government funded, up-to-date data to realize the healthcare goals. A number of researchers have pointed out the lack of health care delivery specific studies.

"While scanning through the available literature on the health status of the tribal women in India, it was observed that comprehensive area specific health related studies were limited; most of the available studies were isolated, fragmentary and did not cover the various dimensions of health, affecting the status of tribal women. (Wilkinson 1992).

Other important co-factors, which have a profound influence on the health of an individual, are one's savings and education.

Savings

Planned financial savings from the income plays an important role in deciding to seek health care in need. In India, post-independent policies by the Government have been framed with a view to encourage savings. A survey conducted by the Indian Post Office in 2002 reveals that India has impressive savings in general. In 1960, India was at 16.7 %, which was much higher than Korea, Singapore and Taiwan at that particular point of time.

According to Abdul Salaam and Umma Kulsum (2002) one of the common reasons for saving is provision for medical need and old age. Personal savings help to a great extent in meeting the expenses of unforeseen health expenses. Utter poverty, in other words, prevent the poor tribals from availing the healthcare benefits.

Table- 2.2

Volume of Savings in India

	1980-81	**%**	**1990-91**	**%**	**1998-99**	**%**
Household savings	21,848	75.9	1,09,623	84.4	3,25,456	82.7
Private savings	2,284	8.0	14940	11.5	67,573	17.2
Public savings	4,654	16.2	5,436	4.2	5,720	0.15
Total savings	28,786	100	1,29,999	100	3,93,601	100

(Economic Survey 1999-2000)

This table indicates that savings in India is on the rise. This is essentially due to the fact that today's planned savings will result in financial buffers to combat health related financial vulnerability. Savings can potentially insulate a person from sudden shock of health care expenses. Among the elite urban mass and the educated rural, a few recognize the strong social purpose behind the planned savings but the poor and particularly the tribals have no knowledge about the concepts and its long-term benefits.

A study conducted on the poor group in Holakere taluk of Chitradruga District of Karnataka by a team from Humboldt University of Germany showed that 60% of the sample population had never made financial savings of any significance in any place (Aloysius Fernandez et al 2005).

This low savings has such a serious impact on health care that the state government has taken note of the situation and is releasing more funds to upgrade the quality of health care systems in the rural areas.

In accordance with the existing laws, the states would sign a Memorandum of Understanding with the Government of India, indicating their commitment to increased contribution to Public Health Budget (preferably by 10% each year), increased devolution to Panchayat Raj Institutions as per 73rd Constitution (Amendment) Act, and performance benchmarks for release of funds (N. R. H. M. Website).

The National Sample Survey in collaboration with the State Directorate of Economics and Statistics conducted a survey of village facilities in Karnataka during July - December 2002. The statistics is as follows.

Table- 2.3

Saving facilities in villages in Karnataka

Facility	Within village	Less than 2 km	2 km to less than 5km	5 km to less than 10 km	10 km or more	All
Metalled road	560	144	274	32	10	1000
Post office	319	159	494	11	16	1000
Telegraph office / PCO	194	39	386	100	281	1000
Bank	89	62	413	157	279	1000

Banks and post offices are the two main centers, which facilitate financial savings for people in India. Difficulty in accessing these centers may sometimes act as a barrier for savings among rural masses.

Education

"............hence education is twice blessed thing – it benefits those who give it and those who receive it" (Jeffrey 1992).

"Literacy is defined in the census of India as the ability to read and write with understanding in any language." The level of literacy is undoubtedly one of the most important indicators of social, cultural and health development of a society in general and neglected section like tribals in particular (Census of India).

It is estimated that globally more than 960 million adults are illiterate, two thirds of whom are women. Studies across the globe suggest that women with a few years of schooling have more self-confidence and contribute effectively to health decisions (Basu 1993).

Most of the literates among the Scheduled Tribes had studied only up to the primary level. Within the country, the level of literacy among the tribals varied widely, reported a status paper for the national workshop on "Status of Tribal Women in India" (National Commission for Women 1993).

All the governments across the globe have initiated schooling programmes considering the urgent need for it. But it appears that social background and consequent responses are barely accommodated into the design of such programmes. "By and large, their response to programmes of literacy and of formal education varied significantly between tribes and from region to region. These responses depended on their socio-cultural, economic and demographic characteristics and on the magnitude and direction of the forces of modernization, such as urbanization and industrialization" (Bose, A.B. 1970).

The Indian tribals have been exposed to literacy only recently (Raza Moonis et al 1990). A large number of tribals are illiterates. Even the present generation tribal children are not able to access the schools in many parts of the country. In rural communities services of school going children are utilized in households, which could possibly affect their span of precious schooling life.

The National Sample Survey in collaboration with the State Directorate of Economics and Statistics conducted a survey of village facilities in Karnataka during July - December 2002. The statistics are as follows:

Table- 2.4
Distribution of various Schools per 1000 villages by distance

Facility	Within village	Less than 2 km	2 km to less than 5km	5 km to less than 10 km	10 km or more	All
Pre-primary schools	741	31	226	-	2	1000
Primary schools	743	31	226	-	-	1000
Middle schools	475	111	368	36	10	1000
Secondary schools	166	80	456	100	198	1000

It is unfortunate that many villages have pre-primary and primary schools which are at a distance of 5 km. Large distances can also be a discouraging factor which prevents young children from going to school.

The tribal children comprising about 15 percent of the total population in India are roughly about 10 million in number who live in such isolated and inaccessible areas (Neti Mahanti 1991).

According to the 1991 census data, excluding Assam, Jammu and Kashmir, the literacy rate among the general population aged 7 years and above was found to be 52.19 (64.20 for males and 39.19 for females). Literacy among the tribals was found to be very low i.e. 25.9 percent and especially so among the tribal females (14.5 percent) (tribalzone.net 1991).

"Among school going children, it is girls who suffer a benefit of regular attendance most. Probably, mothers take help from their daughters most, as mother herself is illiterate." In a Tribal study in Orissa, revealed that girls enrolment is very low compared to boys (Biswal G. C. 1991).

As women do most of the household works, it is but natural that, they utilize the services of their school going children.

"Even today women carry the responsibility of some 80-90 % of house hold chores." (United Nation Report 1991)

The lowest level of literacy among the tribals was recorded in Andhra pradesh [14.5 percent] and the highest in Mizoram[80.0 percent]. The lowest level of literacy among the females was found in Rajasthan [4.1 percent]. Along the tribal territories, the highest literacy among tribals was observed in Lakshadweep[79.1percent]Indian tribes have been exposed to literacy only recently (Moonis Raza, et al., 1990).

Since girls in tribal communities have multiple tasks to perform, it becomes apparent that they do not get sufficient time to concentrate on studies.

Literacy is important for the young girl; it had correlations with the survival of her children. Infant mortality is found to decrease significantly when the mother is educated up to the primary level and above" (Basu, 1993).

In all the societies, the mother is the first teacher. This is not only true for education but also for behavioral actions like discipline and cleanliness. Therefore, the mother's illiteracy will have a direct impact on schooling and general health of tribal children. There are numerous studies to suggest that the influence of paternal literacy on the health status is only about half as strong as that of the mother's education. The status of women in a society is a clear reflection of the level of social justice in that society.

Kelsey A Harrison, Professor of Obstetrics and Gynecology at the University of Port Harcourt in Nigeria says, "Through an educated mother, the cycle of illiteracy and bad health can be broken because her daughters and sons will probably go to school and so would succeeding generations."

World Bank also endorses the view that female education is the most influential instrument with high financial returns. "In India the health of children depends a great deal on the initiative of women," (World Bank Report 2003).

Female education is crucial because "A tribal woman occupies an important place in the socio-economic structure of her society"(Dhebar Commission 1961). "Moreover, the status of tribal women has gone from bad to worse as a result of the impact of social change, which has affected the social structure of tribal society" (Chauhan et al. 1990).

Dyson and Moore (1983) put forth a similar argument. Illiteracy also encourages preference for male children, more so in the poor societies. At times cultural background promotes the concept of preference for male children. Sex selective abortion, although more common in urban areas, is gaining popularity in rural areas too. The thought of begetting male children is predominant and they venture to seek all possible help (Sen et al).

Education has a direct bearing on the quality of life and health is a byproduct of good education. Enrolment of Tribal children to school in elementary school in Karnataka rose from 11.7 to 14.1 millions between 1995 and 2001 according to the Department of Education, Government of Karnataka 2002.

Midtala Rani and Nanjunda D C (2007) observe that the results of formal education programme for tribal children in Karnataka have not been very encouraging. It has failed to remove the sense of alienation, inferiority and pessimism from their hearts. There is a need to adopt non-formal education and to have suitable teachers who can devotedly handle the specially designed educational programme for the tribal people.

The review of literature scrutinized so far suggests that although a large amount of research work on tribal health care is carried out, most of them appear to have dealt with "the poor health of the tribals and the causes" in its entirety. Hardly any work has been undertaken with regard to health care service delivery in specific tribal areas accommodating the views and experiences of all concerned. Other researchers have studied "poor nutritional status" as a precursor of disease and as a center point along with inadequate infrastructure.

Therefore the present study is an effort to understand the shortfalls in the present health care delivery system. This was made possible due to the candidness of all respondents who are concerned like the teachers in the tribal schools and the healthcare professionals in tribal areas. This study varies from others, which have been done so far in many respects. One important feature of the study has been the interviews taken of the tribals themselves. Very valuable information was thus obtained based on which hypotheses could be formed. This is important when one considers that the tribals manage to maintain their own identity even when integrating with new medical systems. Thus this study symbolizes the transition from theoretical saturation to corroborative new insight.

HEALTH CARE SERVICES DELIVERY

The last fragment of the entire healthcare management system is its service delivery. Its success lies when service is delivered in its expected design. A patient's experience while receiving treatment characterizes the quality of health care service delivery. United Nations Millennium Development Goals (MDG) clearly underscores the importance of health care delivery. United Nations General Assembly has accorded the highest priority to reaching health services to the poor. Need based health care services, both in preventive and curative forms, should be a part of the country's poverty reduction strategy. According to David H. Peters et al (2002) the objectives of the Health System and the Health transition are

- Improving the health status of the population, thereby lowering mortality and morbidity rates
- Protecting the population against financial risks while dealing with health problems
- Responding to citizens' demands and needs.

Professor Regina E. Herzlinger(2006) the editor of "Consumer Driven Healthcare" observed that medical treatment has made astonishing advances over the years. But the packaging and the delivery of the treatment are often inefficient, ineffective and consumer unfriendly.

According to Professor Regina E. Herzlinger(2006), there are six forces affecting innovation in health care. They are-

- *Funding* – The processes for generating revenue and acquiring capital, both of which differ from those in most other industries.
- *Public policy* - The regulations that pervade the industry, because incompetent or fraudulent suppliers can do irreversible human damage.
- *Technology* - The foundation for advances in treatment and for innovations that can make health care delivery more efficient and convenient.
- *Customers* - The increasingly engaged consumers of healthcare, for whom the passive term "patients" seems outdated.

- *Accountability* –The demand from vigilant consumers and cost pressured payers that innovative health care products be not only safe and effective but also cost effective relative to competing products.
- *Industry players* - The friends and foes lurking in the health care system that can destroy or bolster an innovation's chance of success.

Today any project on health care management should take into account the quality of delivery and how it reaches the people. No better management person could have explained solution /customer satisfaction than renowned Management Guru Mr. C.K. Prahlad.(2004)

Table- 3.1 Product perspective Vs Solution perspective

	Product perspective	**Solution perspective**
Value proposition	Win by creating innovative products and enriching features of existing products	Win by creating and delivering superior customer solutions
Value creation	Value is created by the firm	Value is co-created by the Customer and the firms
Designing offerings	Start with the product or the service and then target customer segments	Start with the customer problem and then assemble required products and services to solve the problem
Company-customer Relationship	Transaction based	Interaction based and centered on the co-creation of solutions
Focus on quality	Quality of internal processes and company offerings	Quality of customer –firm interactions

(C.K. Prahalad and Venkat Ramaswamy 2004)

In developing countries, it is poverty by and large that leads to poor health condition, and poor health in turn leads to poverty. Poor countries around the world have adopted many strategies recognizing the vicious cycle of poverty and ill health.

India adopted the Alma-Ata declaration in 1978, which called for, "Health for all by the Year 2000". Subsequently, the National Health Policy of 1983 supported a massive expansion of rural health infrastructure – from village to district level. The enthusiasm exhibited by the government in this direction is praiseworthy. But inherent shortcomings in the system prevented the programme from becoming a success. In Indian scenario there is an acute shortage of health care professionals. Then unequal distribution of this invaluable resource compounds the problem. Therefore health care service delivery needs an urgent relook in order to meet the needs of the poor adequately (WHO: 2006).

THE DIMENSIONS OF SERVICE QUALITY

The art of managing the customers, the customer's expectations and aspirations, created through the creative communication strategies. It is all about managing the promises made to customers and promises kept (Zeithaml and Bitner, 2006).

Parasuraman et al (1985) formulated a service quality model that highlights the main requirements for delivering high service quality.

- Gap between consumer expectation and management perception
- Gap between management perception and service quality specification.
- Gap between consumer expectation and management perception: Management does not always correctly perceive what customers want. Hospital administrators may think that patients want better food; but patients may be more concerned about nurse responsiveness.
- Gap between management perception and service-quality specification: Management might correctly perceive customers' wants but not set a performance standard. Hospital administrators may tell the nurses to give "fast" service without specifying it in minutes.
- Gap between service quality specifications and service delivery: personnel might be poorly trained or incapable or unwilling to meet the standard; or they may be have conflicting ideas as to standards, such as whether to take time in serving customers or whether to give them fast service.
- Gap between service delivery and external communications: statements made by company representatives and ads affect consumer expectations. If a hospital brochure shows a beautiful room, but the patient arrives and finds the

room cheap and tacky looking, external communications have distorted the customer's expectations.

- ❖ Gap between perceived service and expected service: This gap occurs when the consumer misperceives the service quality. The physician may keep visiting the patient to show that they care, but the patient may interpret this an indication that something is really wrong.

While improving service productivity, increasing cost may be a concern. Philip Kotler (2004) lists out seven approaches to increase service productivity
Seven approaches to improving service productivity.

- ➢ Have service providers work more skillfully. The company can hire and foster more skillful workers through better selection and training.
- ➢ Increase the quantity of service by surrendering some quality. Doctors working for some HMOs have moved towards handling more patients and giving less time to each patient.
- ➢ "Industrialize the service" by adding equipment and standardizing production.
- ➢ Reduce or make obsolete the need for a service by inventing a product solution, the way wash and wear shirts reduced the need for commercial laundries and the way certain authorities reduced the need for tuberculosis sanitoriums.
- ➢ Design a more effective service. How to quit smoking clinics may reduce the need for expensive medical services later on. Hiring paralegal workers reduces the need for more expensive legal professionals.
- ➢ Present customers with incentives to substitutes their own labor for company labor. Banks have turned their customers into tellers; FedEx has turned customers into shippers; gas stations have turned customers into gas pumpers; and the phone company has turned customers into operators.
- ➢ Harness the power of technology to give customers access to better service and make service workers more productive. Companies that use their web sites to empower customers can lessen workloads, capture valuable data, and increase the value of their business. Technology has great power to make service workers more productive.

Health care service delivery is multidimensional and is not standardized in small towns in general and tribal areas in particular. Therefore there is always a lurking fear in patients (consumer) about service performance, consistency and quality and perception of risk (Valarie A Zeithaml 1981).

The most frequently employed technique is word of mouth to assess the quality of service in rural set ups. Further, it is very difficult to evaluate the process of services tendered, as it is abstract, random and symptoms-dependent.

Some insight can be drawn as to how consumers evaluate service quality from the following table:

Table 3.2 Dimensions of Service Quality

Dimension	Description	Examples
Reliability	Delivering on promises	Promised delivery date met
Responsiveness	Being willing to help	Prompt reply to customers' request
Assurance	Inspiring trust and confidence	Professional and knowledgeable staff
Empathy	Treating customers as individuals	Adapts to special needs of customer
Tangibles	Representing the service physically	Distinctive material brochures, documents

(Valarie A Zeithaml, Mary jo Bitner and Dwayne D. Gremler, services Marketing Integ rating Customer focus across the firm. 4 th ed.(Boston : McGraw –Hill Irwin,2006),pp.116-120)

According to the above-mentioned table, consumer focus is on five dimensions (Reliability, Responsiveness, Assurance, Empathy and Tangibles) in evaluating service quality. Among these, reliability - delivering on promises - is the most important factor. Here the frontline service provider assumes a great importance (Valarie A Zeithaml 2006).

Given the uniqueness in the customer pattern, that is. each patient coming with different symptoms of diseases, services need to be customized. An employee (health care professional) who feels that personal worth results only from self sacrificing work or occupational achievement would be likely to derive some satisfaction even in a demanding menial position (Blood et al 1969).

It is unlikely that the expectations of the customer are met if service patterns are routine. Need and expectation of the customer will differ inter and intra individually from time to time. Segmentation of services in order to customize will also lead to effective utilization of resources. Therefore, the service provided can be thought to be a "Service Package". Service package would consist of product dimension of service, including decisions about the essential concept of the service, the range of services provided and the quality and the level of services provided. In addition, the service package must consider some unique factors –the personnel who perform the service, the physical product that accompanies the service and the process of providing the service.

Chart -3.1
Summary of Model Theories: Focus and Key Concepts

	Theory	Focus	Key concepts
Individual Level	Stages of Change Model	Individual's readiness to change or attempt to change toward healthy behaviours	Precontemplation Contemplation Decision/determination Action Maintenance
	Health Belief Model	Person's perception of the threat of a health problem and the appraisal of recommended behaviour(s) for preventing or managing the problem	Perceived susceptibility Perceived severity Perceived benefits of action Cues to action Self-efficacy
Interpersonal Level	Social Learning Theory	Behaviour is explained via a 3-way, dynamic reciprocal theory in which personal factors, environmental influences and behaviour continually interact	Behaviour capability Reciprocal determinism Expectations Self-efficacy Observational learning Reinforcement
Community Level	Community Organisation Theories	Emphasises active participation and development of communities that can better evaluate and solve health and social problems	Empowerment Community competence Participation and relevance Issue selection Critical consciousness
	Organisational Change Theory	Concerns processes and strategies for increasing the chances that healthy policies and programmes will be adopted and maintained in formal organisations	Problem definition (awareness stage) Initiation of action (adoption stage) Implementation of change Institutionalisation of change
	Diffusion of Innovations Theory	Addresses how new ideas, products and social practices spread within a society or from one society to another	Relative advantage Compatibility Complexity Trialability Observability

Chart -3.2

Service quality model

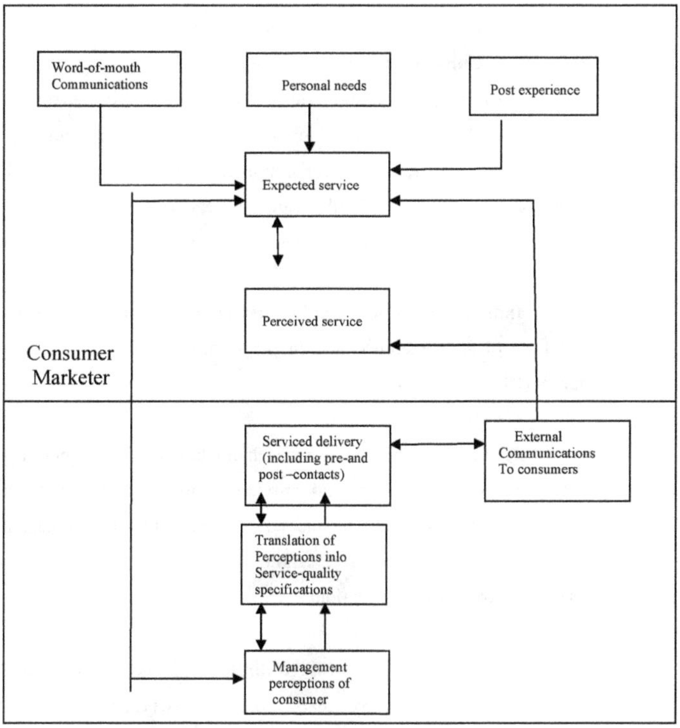

Source: A.Parasuraman, Valarie A Zeithaml, and Leonard L Berry ,A conceptual model of service quality and its implications for future research, Services marketing (New York McGraw-Hill, 1996, Ch 2

HEALTH CARE INFRASTRUCTURE IN INDIA

Management of Health care Services Delivery consists of components namely

(a) Infrastructure

(b) Human Resource

(a) Infrastructure

The Infrastructure includes hospital building, a wide range of degradable and replaceable elements starting from selection of technology, which is followed by the selection of company, brands, design, make, cost, maintenance, transportation, etc. The physical infrastructure includes hospitals, clinics, nursing homes, teaching institutes, laboratories, etc. and the human infrastructures include doctors, nurses, and other supporting staffs. Health care delivery system can function when health care centers are adequately manned with doctors, nurses and other supporting staffs.

India's current health policy has its origins in the nation-building activities at the time of Independence and in the thinking embodied in the Bhore Committee report (Bhore et al. 1946).

A focus on existing service channels and its distribution to meet the health care need of the tribals would provide an insight into the desired output services levels. This does also help us understand, constraints and suggest alternative channels if needed. While providing Health care is the ultimate objective, infrastructure assumes a role as its foundation.

According to The World Health Report (WHO: 2006) "Health care is a labour-intensive service industry that number of workers and quality are positively associated".

A greater insight into how to bring about a successful health care service delivery does hinge on a wide range of elements like the physical layout of the meeting room, ambience, accessibility, approach, environment, equipment, responsiveness, attitude and flexibility.

It would be apt to aim at specific and need based policies to be effective in health care system. For example, rural masses find it difficult to access the benefit of health care due to physical distance.

While the Primary Health Centre is expected to be manned by the full staff, one male and one female health multipurpose worker is the norm for sub centre and, for tribal areas, 1 female worker for 6 sub -centers.

Table- 3.3 Medical Staff in Health Centers

	P.H.C	Sub Center
Plain Area	30000	5000 (1Female + 1Male Multipurpose)
Tribal area	20000	3000 (1Female for 6 centers)

As per the Rural Health Infrastructure Bulletin 2006, there was a shortage of 19,269 Sub-Centres (SCs), 4,337 Primary Health Centres (PHCs) and 3,206 Community Health Centres (CHCs) as per 2001 population norm. Further, almost 50 per cent of the existing health infrastructure was in rented buildings. Last but not the least, poor upkeep and maintenance and high absenteeism of manpower in rural areas have eroded the credibility of the health delivery system in the public sector.

In an effort to fill the vacancies in Primary Health Centres (PHCs), the Government has recently empowered the Deputy Commissioners to make appointments on contract basis. The Government is also considering policy amendments to encourage private participation in Primary Health Centres (Poverty and Human Development 2002-03).

A research paper brought out by Dr Milind Deogaonkar (2004) deals with the fact that pre-existing inequality in the healthcare provisions is further enhanced by difficulties in accessing it. These difficulties can be due to

1. Geographical distance
2. Socio-economic distance
3. Gender distance

As discussed earlier, in rural areas, even a basic care is inaccessible to the vast majority of people. The difficulty to access the health care is further compounded by inadequate number of health care professionals. "Thousands of primary medical centers exist, but they are perpetually short of personnel and medicines." (Naseem Shah 2004)

The following table indicates that health care centers are least in number in Karnataka compared to other three southern states.

Table- 3.4
Comparison of Health Care Facilities in Southern States of India

	Primary Health Care Centre	**Sub centres**	**Community health centres in Thousands**	**Population per bed**
India	27364	4579	214	1498
Andhra Pradesh	29719	4601	204	1526
Tamilnadu	25614	4237	511	1120
Kerala	22311	4205	267	391
Karnataka	18537	3815	124	1283

(Bulletin on Rural Health Statistics in India, June 2002)

Health care professionals have to travel long distances and are away from their families for long periods. Poor transportation to work place and inadequate facilities can negatively affect the quality of service.

Sherry (1991) suggested that a poor "person-environment fit" results in lowered performance and productivity.

Poverty and ill-health nexus is a very old and well-known problem. Search is on for lasting solutions to deal with that problem with the available new technology, knowledge and resources at our disposal. However the application of managerial dimension to tackle the health care threat has been injected only recently. As a result of the changed phenomenon our country began to witness certain positive changes in this sector. For instance, there has been an impressive growth in the number of hospitals in our country between 1991 to year 2000. The number of hospitals grew from 11,174 in 1991 (57% private) to 18,218 (75% private) in 2000 (Health Information of India 2000&2001).

Pradhana Mantri Swasthya Suraksha Yojana (PMSSY) has increased the financial outlay from Rs 9253 crore- to Rs10252 crore to upgrade hospitals in the country, recognizing the urgent health care need.

Total metalled road in Karnataka is 134062 kms. which shows 70 km of availability of roads for every 100 square kms of geographical area. The average length of metalled roads for each taluka is 766 kms. Nearly 85 taluks where length of road per 100 sq kms of area is less than 32 kms have to be considered for further connectivity of roads (Sixth Five Year Plan GOI).

The approach in India was unlike that of high-income former British colonies such as Canada and Australia. Over time, only countries that have had the political and social support for such systems have been able to maintain the high levels of public investment in health. More than 5 percent of gross domestic product [GDP] is necessary to sustain them (Peters et al. 2002).

India has witnessed market reforms in all sectors including health sector in the recent years. The aim of these market reforms is to stimulate the market economy in general. It is also expected that benefits of this global phenomenon reach all. But uniform accrual of health care benefits did not happen across urban and rural India. Distinctions are evident between urban and rural health care sectors with respect to infrastructure and modern diagnostic equipment. Urban areas have benefited more than the rural areas. Even among the urban population, the rich have benefited far more than the poor.

Given below is the plan of Medical & Public Health and social services by the Government of Karnataka. It can be observed that actual expenditure on health care did exceed the budget outlay suggesting growing expenditure of health care.

Table- 3.5
Medical & Public Health and Social Services Tenth Plan -2002-07
(Government of Karnataka)

	Approved Outlay Medical and Public Health	Revised Outlay Medical and Public Health	Actual Expenditure Medical and Public Health	Social Services
Annual Plan - 2002-03	19247.00	19948.00	17715.31	43798.00
Annual Plan - 2003-04	13974.00	16884.66	19189.66	55382.94
Annual Plan - 2004-05	18011.51	15731.51	15731.51	90615.59
Annual Plan - 2005-06	33239.29	28920.80	N.A	95986.18
Annual Plan - 2006-07	34098.61	N.A.	N.A.	95361.68

Commutation to the work place becomes very difficult with poor infrastructure. Managing with the poor infrastructure in rural area builds up a great deal of stress among the health care professionals.

Many big business houses have been attracted to the health care business. As a result, a number of private hospitals have begun to spring up in the length and breadth of our country. Many taluk head quarters also have begun to witness this phenomenon. Again these facilities remain a dream for the rural poor due to the high cost of treatment. Therefore, once again these facilities cater to the health care needs of the rich only.

According to Dr. Nirmala Murthy (2006) Honorary President, Foundation for Research in Health Systems, Bangalore, "Private services are too expensive for them (poor). They therefore resort to care in the unregulated informal sector, which is of questionable quality, which makes them vulnerable to higher health risk."

A study conducted by Hanagodimath S V et al shows that there are disparities in education and health indexes among various states. Growth of number of Allopathic Hospitals, Dispensaries and PHC's also important health infra structures like number of doctors and nurses. The number of dispensaries per million populations was 16.6 in the year 1971 which increased to 35.1 in the year 1989 but started to decrease from the year 1999 (34.5 per million populations in 1989 to 22 per million populations in 2001) (Sixth Five Year Plan, Government of India).

The national sample survey in collaboration with the state Directorate of Economics and Statistics conducted a survey of 176 villages on infrastructure facilities during July –December 2002 in Karnataka. The survey found that as many as 38 % of all villages in Karnataka had to travel more than 5 km to reach the nearest dispensary, the most peripheral contact point in the government primary health care system. Also 44% of the villages were more than 5 km away from the nearest primary health centre. For 50% of the villages in the state the nearest government hospital was more than 10 km away. Private hospitals were most scarce, the nearest one being more than 10 km away for 54.5 % of the villages. The problem of resources is not merely confined to their inadequacies; it has to do with their distribution as well. 73 rd amendment of Indian constitution has given constitutional status to rural local bodies in India (Dir. of Econ. and Stat. Infra. Kar. 2002).

"The particular aspect of the problem noted in empirical studies is the massive diversion of rural health care services to family planning campaigns." (Iyengar and Bhargava 1987 prakasamma 1989, Gupta et al 1992).

"The ratio of hospital beds to population in rural areas is fifteen times lower than that for urban areas in Karnataka. The ratio of doctors to population in rural areas is almost six times lower than that in the urban population."

The following table explains the facilities available in number of villages in Karnataka

Table 3.6
Facilities available in villages in Karnataka

Facilities Available in Karnataka	Percentage of Villages
Primary Health centre	**10.1 %**
Medical Shops	**7.9 %**
Govt Hospital	**2.7 %**
Veterinary Hospital	**13.5 %**
Facility for disabled	**Very poor**

The private clinic or doctor was more readily available. This facility existed in more than 19.5 % of state villages (M.B. Nanjappa).

According to Mr. M.B. Nanjappa, formerly Director of Economics and Statistics, Karnataka, "Even today many basic items are dearer in rural areas of Karnataka like medical care, water supply and sanitation. Their diet is poor and there are risks of early death particularly among infants".

Burgeoning but unregulated private healthcare sector makes the gap between rich and poor more apparent. In this regard it is appropriate to have a glimpse of the current scenario with respect to medical care available in India. Though modern well-equipped hospitals both in the government and private sectors are available to the people, the concentration seems to be in urbanized India, thereby leaving a huge gap between rural and urban India's accessibility to health care. It would be note worthy at this juncture to counter the high cost of health care through a more holistic form of health care system, which we call indigenous or traditional medical system. Initially, the tribals had their own system of medical system to. Not surprisingly, the poor not only suffer a loss of income when they are sick, they have to bear higher insecurity from the illness and the high cost of healthcare services.

Shankar Acharya in his article "Governance and Health" says that while in general, Kerala shows performances comparable to more advanced states in terms of some indicators, other states like Bihar and Uttar Pradesh present a grim picture. Therefore there are great inter and intravariations in the health care delivery systems in our country,

Role of Transportation and Speed of Services

Transportation serves as a bridge between networks of logistic services. Lack of effective and adequate transportation system will question the effectiveness of service delivery. Although cost appears to be a major barrier for effective and timely transportation, the objective must be to save human life and not cost per se. Cost advantage philosophy can be harsh and must be carefully employed weighing the benefit and risk ratio. Very often cost of service is linked to performance of service. The cost of service is a variable depending on need and the type of service. Therefore, the mode of transportation has to be justified and has to be relative to the objective to be achieved. Cost becomes immaterial in times of emergency.

Speed of Service- Lapse of time in transportation can result in failure to achieve the objective of saving precious human life. Reduction of distance ensures that only service consistency need be monitored. Consistency differs with different modes of transportation. This variation in consistency is to be taken into account, while designing service delivery system. Average transit time, consistency, urgency (need) must determine the mode of transportation. In short, the need of the hour determines the mode of transport system – whether ordinary or expedited.

Broadly all available health care centers can be put into three categories, namely, governmental health care sector, private health care sector and NGO sector. All of them have varied commercial interests in treating patients along with their organizational vision and mission. Patients perceive services provided by different health care sectors differently. The providers of health care services include mainly the doctors, the nurses, the midwives and other supportive paramedical staffs like the laboratory assistant, the ambulance assistant etc.

Government Health Care Sector

This is the sector where almost all poor patients visit to seek redressal to their medical problem. This sector outnumbers the other two sectors due to the resources at its disposal. This sector operates on a very large scale. While some degree of accountability is maintained in the services, poor managerial disbursement of resources leaves the patients dissatisfied. Given the very size of the organization certain competency standards are maintained. However, insensitive approach and crude behavior towards the poor patients repulse the poor. Most of its health budget is utilized in utter disregard of the priorities like service delivery.

Private Health Care Sector

This sector differs from its counterpart in its built in philosophy of return on investment (ROI). Corporate health care sectors are accountable to shareholders for its profitable operations. Private sectors employ professional marketers to remain closer to the patients. Overall discipline is more acceptable to patients in this sector. But it has limitations in terms of competency and accountability because health service employees are attracted by higher pay packages. Medium and small players in Private sectors may face resource crunch as medical field is ever advancing. Therefore, it is difficult for the patients to assess the quality of overall service delivery. The opening up of economy witnessed the growth of private healthcare sector in India. But it also played a role in increasing the existing social divide. The cost of medical treatment is so high in the private sector that it denies access to poorer sections of society. With profitability overriding service philosophy, these modern health care centers are urban-biased. Return on Investment remains a motto in large corporate hospitals. This ever-increasing cost of healthcare has making healthcare unaffordable for a growing number of poor people.

NGO Health Care Sector

Sensitivity to the needs of the poor and quality care is integrated into the healthcare service delivery in this sector. Good characters and people of social standing distinguish this sector from others. NGO health care sectors enjoy a good reputation of providing health care to the poor. Resources limit its reach to different rural areas. In delivering the health care services to the poor, these organizations have ample scope to be innovative and to implement efficiently. In other words, the strengths of these organizations lie exactly in areas where the government is weak.

It would be an efficient combined resource if both the government and the NGO organizations join hands in a constructive partnership. Both the sectors have organizational strengths, which are complementary to each other. Rapid climatic changes are occurring due to a number of factors. Some of them are unavoidable. Rapid deforestation, swift urbanization, drifting away from age-old food habits to mention a few, have potential catalytic effect on epidemiological diseases.

(b) Human Resource

Although physical and human infrastructures of health sector are complementary to each other for the development of health care delivery system as a whole, the human component has a greater importance.

Lee Jong-Wook (2006) recognized that the most important crisis in the health sector is the crisis in human resources.

The human side will continuously upgrade the skills and knowledge to formulate plans, strategies and design to effectively manage and deliver the benefits of services. This could be an interesting topic to researchers considering the dynamic nature of the systemic delivery at work place. Another feature of the topic is that although the focus would be on design, the emphasis is on delivery path. With the availability of newer and upgraded technology, its utility can be reached to the poor and the downtrodden only with the retention, motivation and on job satisfaction of the health care professionals.

It is no surprise that developed countries have placed health on highest priority. Although all governments across the globe feel the same need, it is the planning and delivery of health care system, which distinguishes the poor from the rich nations. Consequently numbers of health care professionals are impressively high in developed countries.

According to Prof. Sailabala Debi (2008), "The average density of health care professionals moves in unison with the development status of the countries of the world, i.e., more developed - higher density, less developed - lower density and so on".

It is a general presumption that the countries with higher burden of diseases need more health care professionals than the countries with lower burden of diseases. But contrary to this, it is found that the countries with lower needs have higher number of health care professionals and the countries with higher needs have fewer numbers of health care professionals. Unreasonable over- concern about health care in developed countries for their citizens has resulted in polarization of resources.

The average density of health care professionals shows that the highly developed countries have about ten times (9.8) more health care professionals than that in less developed countries (1.7). The mean density (4.6) of health care professionals in medium developed countries is nearly half of that in highly developed countries. Both the medium developed and less developed countries are below the all-countries' average of health care professionals while the highly developed countries are above the all-countries' average density of health care professionals.

Speybroeck N et.al (2006) observed, "Region of the America, which includes Canada and the United States, contains only 10% of the global burden of disease, yet almost 37% of the world's health workers live in this region and spend more than 50% of the world's financial resources for health. In contrast, the African Region suffers more than 24% of the global burden of disease but has access to only 3% of health workers and less than 1% of the world's financial resources – even with loans and grants from abroad.

This is a clear indication of the importance attached to health of the citizens by developed countries, which in turn is the indicator of the health of the country. In contrast, we do not even have an access to basic health care facilities in our country for the poor. These components play a key role in determining the soundness and the efficiency of the health care system.

With the apparent poor ratio of health professionals to population, the health care delivery system would be thrown out of gear. There is a repeated warning from World Health Organization that metabolic disorders like diabetes and hypertension (slow killing diseases) are on the rise in India.

According to Dr. Nirmala Murthy (2006), in 2000, India had 1.25 million doctors and 0.8 million nurses. That translates into one doctor for every 1800 people. If other systems including Indigenous System of Medicine (ISM) and homeopathic medicine are considered, there is one doctor per 800 people. Public services, which are free for the poor, are poorly staffed and equipped and therefore cannot provide good quality services to the poor.

The rural health problem that our country is facing is much bigger than it has been projected. Although approximately 15,000 new graduate doctors and 5,000 postgraduate doctors are trained every year it is not translated into bridging the gap of demand and supply of health care professionals. Our country has a very impressive annual pharmaceutical production of about 260 billion (INR). Pharmaceutical companies are encouraged to manufacture large quantum due to inexpensive workforce and government subsidy. But again a large proportion of these medicines are exported (Ministry of Chemicals 2002).

The government has promised to increase health care services for the rural areas and the poor by appointing community health workers, and implementing a national insurance program - but little has been done so far to meet those goals. Poor health conditions can be a major source of capability deprivation and hence a cause for unemployment and poverty.

In this context it is interesting to note a quote from Harvard Business School (May 2006). "From a financial perspective a physician who is paid a fat salary by a health maintenance organization may be less interested in say performing a procedure to implant a monitoring device than would a doctor who is paid a fee for such services."

Resource planning assumes utmost importance to put an efficient system in place. Health care is not an exception. More investments on human resources in the health sector particularly in less developed countries are urgently needed. The broad categories of health care may be preventive provided health care services are delivered in time. When this fails, the poor have to resort to curative care of the advanced state of the disease.

Preventive care includes immunization/vaccination for different communicable diseases, ensuring nutrition of children and mothers, etc. Promotive care includes sanitation, water supply and information about different health awareness programmes. Curative care may be classified as hospital care and ambulatory care. Hospital care requires the patient to be admitted into the hospital (In Patients). Ambulatory care on the other hand includes all types of routine checkup (Out Patients) and ancillary services.

But this challenge requires humane and managerial capacities as much as or more than financial and physical resources. Even if low income countries train and produce enough doctors or try to import them, they still won't have the economic capacity to pay their wages to retain them It would be better to provide effective health care to the rural population, especially the disadvantaged groups including women and children, by improving access, enabling community ownership and demand for services, strengthening public health systems for efficient service delivery, enhancing equity and accountability and promoting decentralization. Several NGO programs have demonstrated that integrated preventive and curative care that includes access to nutrition, water supply, sanitation, information, preventive care and curative treatment, results in substantial health gains for the poor. In most western countries the knowledge of indigenous medicine is absent or to a great extent it is ignored. This is because western medicine is dependent on allopathic system. Less developed countries still depend on indigenous medicine for providing health care. It is perhaps appropriate to quote the reasons for ignoring traditional medicine.

"In most developing countries the evolution of health services was dominated by western health care models. These have rarely taken into account the way in which local people explain illness and use traditional healing methods" (Wright and Walleye 1998).

Perhaps it would be appropriate to study the entire tribal culture primarily to understand native cures for illnesses and their use of different herbs in spite of not having had a formal education.

"World Health Report (2005) seeks to explain why progress in maternal and child health has apparently stumbled so badly in many countries. It shows in detail how stagnations, reversals and slow progress in some countries are clearly related to poverty, HIV/AIDS, and humanitarian crises, leading to exclusion from access to health care. In many countries, the strategies put in place to provide health services have not produced the expected results. While many countries have based their health care systems on health districts, with a backbone of health centers and a referral district hospital, there has often been a failure to implement this model successfully in an exceedingly resource-constrained context. The chapter argues that the health district model still stands as a rational way for governments to organize decentralized health care delivery .

Job satisfaction and Employee motivation

Effective delivery of organizational objectives and job satisfaction of the employees are the two sides of the same coins. Although there are numerous studies conducted on job satisfaction there is no direct evidence to show whether job satisfaction is a dependent or an independent variable.

According to Ronan (1970 a) job satisfaction is something, which is highly diverse in its definition, influenced by many situational factors, hierarchic specific and depending on individual backgrounds.

Kornhauser (1930) was first to recognize "job satisfaction" as an independent area of management science and is worthy of research who stated:

Blair B (1964) found that the most important job characteristics as satisfiers were interesting duties, job securities and self-actualization.

It would be relevant to know about employee satisfaction in this context. According to Philip Kotler (2004) "Satisfaction is a feeling of pleasure or disappointment resulting from comparing a products perceived performance (or outcome) in relation to his/her expectation".

If the performance falls short of expectation the customer is dissatisfied. if the performance matches the expectation the customer is satisfied and if the performance exceeds expectation the customer is highly satisfied or delighted. (David Glanmick 1999).

Both experts in management science and psychologists are concerned about stress at work place. Stress factor is a practical problem, which needs an urgent redressal without which it can prove costly. A matter of concern is the lower productivity induced by stress on job.

Stress has been shown to reduce employee motivation and the physical ability to perform a task well. This may result in lower production levels and increased errors and accidents (Schultz and Schultz 1990).

The available evidence suggests that job stress contributes to health related problems among employees and organizational problems such as employee dissatisfaction, alienation, absenteeism, and turnover (Beehr and Newman 1978).

The emphasis here is on changes to be made to ensure congenial environment through improved infrastructure for better productivity and not so much on psychological and emotional well being.

"Vocational selection procedures, training programmes, and rest periods are evaluated in terms of efficiency. Why not also to references to satisfaction? Of course the two are not independent; often a study of morale is highly significant in its bearing on output. But even where it is not, we may be interested in the individual and social effects of the work "(Kornhauser A. W 1930).

Enough research is available on the view that service that provides happiness and satisfaction in their job leads to customer satisfaction (Rosenbluth et al. 1991).

Motivation is an important aspect to be considered without which desirable productivity may not be possible to achieve. Peterson et al. (1983) suggested a causal model that comes close to encompassing a number of factors from a variety of disciplines. There are whole ranges of factors in an enterprise that affect the effectiveness of the organization. The factors may be categorized as those pertaining to individuals, the organization and environment. The human error model takes into account both a system failure and a human error.

A number of researchers have studied variables like work satisfaction, behavior, stress versus personality, attentiveness, sleep disorders, aggression behavior modification & classification of human error. Winsemius (1969) studies the tidiness-untidiness continuum in relation to work behaviour, which can be used to analyze not only the skill of the worker but also his psychological adjustment.

Kollarik (1977) analyzed relationship between work satisfaction and various types of work behavior such as job changing, productivity, ego involvement and absenteeism.

Mc Kelvey Robert (1973) investigated attentiveness in a simulated work environment under various incentive conditions and found that a balanced presentation of positive and negative incentive increased the subject's-role awareness without significantly sacrificing performance efficiency.

Customer -benefit Services

A visit to a professionally managed hospital like Narayan Hridayalaya, Bangalore, gives an idea as to how patients across whole spectrum of society, from the poor to the affluent class, derive solution to their health care problems.

In this context customer satisfaction through solutions is best described by Mohanbir Sawhney who writes, "Solutions offer many more avenues for differentiations than products because they include a variety of services that can be customized in many unique ways for individual customers".

A patient's loyalty can be protected and increased when there is a rich network of relationship. Resource planning is a great tool in shaping the services to be perceived in a manner that the customer (patient) at any given point does not switch over to unscientific centers.

According to Henry Assael, services are deeds, processes and performances. The most important difference between goods and services is intangibility as services are actions or performances which cannot be touched or seen in the way that consumers sense tangible goods. But in Health Care Service both goods (equipments and medicine) and services are important. In its conventional form they are separate entities but in this research work both goods and services go hand in hand. Here patients receive medicine, beds, and ambulance availability as goods and courteous personal, quick check up and hospital ambience as services. This can be viewed as "total market offering" (Arun Sharma et al. 2001).

From this perspective, effectiveness of Service delivery depends on how the individual service provider interacts with patients (consumer). Thus actual delivery of services takes place depending on whether promises are kept up or broken.

According to Michael D.Hutt and Thomas W. Speh, (2007). the critical point of interactive contact with a customer is real time marketing. Quality of the services delivered is judged by the patients. Here the patient's perception about the term "quality" has little relevance. According to patients (consumer), good service is whether service provided to him/her meets or exceeds his expectations (William H. Davidow and Bro Uttal 1989).

Therefore it is imperative that all the services in its design and execution should be carefully done. Uniformity of services need not necessarily be consistent as the quality of delivery is not process driven. It can also be that the quality of service output may vary each time. Variation could be in terms of human resources, equipments, labour, and expertise.

Each patient is different hence a significant human element is involved in executing a quality service. Due to this ununiformity envisaged, it calls for a high degree of quality control programmes in delivering health care services. These programmes need to be fine-tuned from time to time by carefully routing the resources to minimize the human error. Keeping this in view, strategy can be formulated to evaluate the existing services.

The core theme of any such move would be to develop customer (patient) centered concept of health care service delivery. It is needless to state that the core benefit and the resultant patients' benefit need to be evaluated periodically. The functional effectual and psychological elements have to be ingrained in the systems.

Customer-benefit service concept involves the complete benefit that a patient derives through a bundle of goods and services. This concept of service must shape the strategies of health care service delivery. Although service concepts are different from industry to industry, the focal point is customer-satisfaction. Service concepts are channeled further to service-offer, which defines in more details when where and to whom the services are provided and its form of presentation (Michael D.Hutt and Thomas W. speh. 2007).

An important phase of product service is the delivery system. This means how the consumer receives the benefits of the service system. The delivery system includes carefully conceived jobs for people: personnel with capabilities and attitude necessary for successful performance: equipment, facilities and layouts for effective customer workflow: and carefully developed procedures and processes aimed at a common set of objectives.

Cronin and Taylor (1992), suggest in their paper "Measuring Service Quality Re-examination" based on global examination of service quality said that

- Grater sharing of information with all connected limbs and customers
- Greater emphasis on process flexibility
- Necessity to co-ordinate the process from all service ends so that help is always available to the customers - competitive pressure to introduce new services and products
- Quick response to customers' needs
- Product and customization

There have been several reform attempts in health care system in India in the last two decades. Market reforms have led to a boom in health sector too. Higher remuneration and facilities have potentially diverted talented practitioners to the private sector creating a larger disparity in the quality of health care. The fast pace of development of the private medical sector and the burgeoning middle class in the new millennium have led to the emergence of a new concept in India of establishing hospitals and health care facilities on a pro-profit basis. Although the importance attached to the health care sector is an appreciable move, uniform health policy may not be a suitable solution for our country. Decentralization and market reform has increased prosperity in general but resulted in increased disparity in wealth and health care access.

The government has developed many health care programmes for the rural poor. But often too many programmes incorporated into single delivery point may not be feasible in the rural set up. Yet another issue, which is diluted, is that formal counseling has never been a part of our health care service delivery in rural areas. It is observed in several studies that the integration of health services with family planning programs often causes the rural population to perceive the primary health centers as hostile to their traditional preference for large families. This perception can make patients to visit health care centres with pre-conceived notions. Therefore primary health centers often play an adversarial role in local efforts to implement national health policies. This can be a hurdle to reach the benefits to the poor. Intentions of egalitarian distribution receive a setback.

Developing countries are faced with severe challenges in the health care delivery mechanism. The emerging market forces in the health sector along with shrinking of public funds to this sector not only affect the delivery mechanism but also lower the quality of health care in the public sector. But a practical problem in providing such a package of services is non-availability of healthcare providers and competent program managers willing to serve in remote, backward areas.

From time to time, the government has tried to meet this staff requirement by making one-year rural service compulsory for medical graduates but that has not been a satisfactory solution. It does not guarantee their performance. The two main pitfalls affecting our ability to provide services to the poor are: (i) corruption and (ii) negative attitudes of health staff towards the poor. (Nirmala Murthy 2006)

Following is the account taken from the compilation by Dr Sailabala Debi (2008) in "Spatial Distribution of Health Workforce and Health Care Services".

"It is disheartening to note that the public expenditure on health in India (0.9% of GDP) is even lower than what the low-income countries (1.1% of GDP) spend on health. Karnataka state's spending (0.7 % of GDP) on health is less than that of India" (Sailabala Debi 2008).

A total of 152 countries of the World were classified as High, Medium and Low on the basis of Human Devolvement Index. There are 48, 64 and 40 countries respectively under high, medium and less developed countries.

Table 3.7 Total and Public Expenditure on Health in Different Countries

Total and Public Expenditure on Health (Exp as % to GDP) and HWF * in different countries			
Countries	**Total exp on Health**	**Public exp on health**	**Av. Density of HWF**
Low income	4.7	1.1	1.7
Middle Income	5.9	3.1	4.6
High Income	11.2	6.7	9.78
India	5.0	0.9	0.30
Karnataka	2.5	0.7	0.36
Source: For LI, MI and HI countries, World Development Indicators, 2007			
India; NHA, Govt of India, 2005, Karnataka: CMDR study on NHA, 2007, HDR report, Govt of Karnataka			

HWF* -Number of health workforce

Recent analyses show that higher absenteeism, low quality in clinical care, low satisfaction level with care (clinical with regard to courtesy and amenities) and rampant corruption plague the system in the public sector (Das and Hammer, 2007).

The variability in quality of health care is on account of many factors, one of which is attributed to health manpower. From all the above discussions it is very clear that the role of health workforce in influencing the health care services in general and in the backward regions in particular assumes great significance.

Health care services have several dimensions. These are mainly physical, human and financial. As discussed earlier, physical and human resources are two basic inputs for production of health output. But these two cannot be utilized without the help of financial resources. So far as the financial dimension is concerned three important questions are raised: Who pays? How much? And for what? (WHO 2003).

The poor in rural set up expect essential health services to be made available at a price they can afford. Dejected with the unfriendly system, the poor want a health system that respects them and is accountable. Poverty has made them aware of the fact that they need protection from adverse impacts of economic policies. The rapid growth of the private sector's entry into the health sector and, at the same time, the absence of doctors, nurses and midwives in public sector have been a growing concern as far as the poor are concerned.

The well-known problems in the government health care services range from filling of the posts, frequent transfers of the health workforce in the public sector to the exodus of health personnel from the public sector to the private sectors. Despite the well-intended outlay by the government, these uncontrollable factors affect the delivery system in the health sector significantly. In the context of less developed countries, the health workforce largely affects all types of health care services.

The average density of Health Work Force (HWF) is found to be slightly higher for Karnataka than for India but the co-efficient of variation for Karnataka (53%) is higher than that for India (40%). This implies that the distribution of health workforce across different districts in Karnataka is more uneven than that in India. It is interesting to note that despite the low density of workforce both in India and Karnataka, the distribution of health workforce in different regions of India and Karnataka is less uneven than that in HD countries.

The following chart provides the association between the expenditure on health and the number of workforce in different countries.

Diagram-3.1 Expenditure on health and number of workforce in different countries

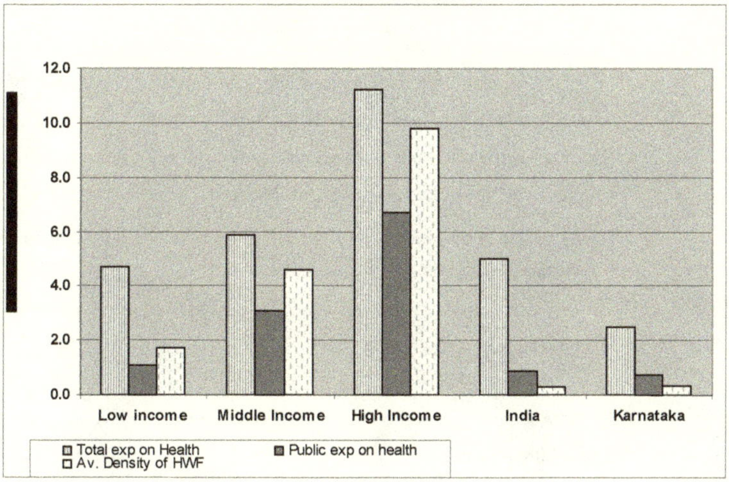

Dr. Sailabala Debi (2008) estimated the geographical variation in the distribution of health workforce across different states of India and across different districts of Karnataka state with the help of Mean, SD and Co-efficient of Variation. The following table presents the Mean, SD and CV of health workforce for India and Karnataka.

Table- 3.8 Variation in Health Workforce: India and Karnataka

Variation in Health Workforce: India and Karnataka		
Descriptive Statistics	India	Karnataka
Mean	0.30	0.36
SD	0.12	0.19
CV (%)	40.00	52.77

Consistent with the recommendations of the World Development Report of 1993, the following health care delivery programmes have been envisaged in our country to help the rural poor by government of India.

- Reviving licentiate medical practitioners to fill the staff vacancies,
- Involving panchayat raj institutions in planning and monitoring health programs,
- Partnering with NGOs in service delivery, regulating private sector
- Increasing the government's health budget to ensure adequate supplies and maintenance.

Adequate funds are the main requirement to achieve this goal of serving the poor by implementing the policy. It is with this view that World Development Report of 1993 recommended that instead of the government directly providing services to the poor, it should use public funds to provide subsidies to non-government organizations that serve the poor and to give the poor the choice of different service providers. One more important feature of the report was to promote public financing of essential clinical services for the poor as a way of reducing poverty.

There is no dearth of literature to suggest that universal access to health care can be achieved through social insurance. Two options can be explored to reach the objective of access of health care for the poor. These options can be-

Management of social insurance with public-private partnership

Public and private services can be integrated to strengthen the service delivery structure preferably in a set up of community-based organization that would manage with utmost care in the interest of the poor rural patients.

Government subsidy or regulation

Government subsidy can address issues like rapid increases in healthcare costs, inefficiency in the system, and shortage of health care professionals, discriminatory access to health care services, etc.

All under-developed and developing countries are plagued with the problem of universal access of health care. In the last two decades there has been considerable debate on this important social issue. There was also widespread call for privatization of public health care. But it is interesting to note that no country has accepted the concept of privatization and reduced its commitment to public health care.

Although in the early 80's many developing countries were facing similar problems as India, many countries prioritized the healthcare issue and its universal access. Think tanks in these countries realized that problems had arisen because of flaws in the financing and regulatory systems. They streamlined the system by reforming their financing and regulatory systems and implemented compulsory social insurance.

General revenues finance public health services in our country. Public health care services are supposed to be free for the poor. Studies on the contrary have shown that the poor do not get free services; they in fact bear disproportionately higher burden of healthcare spending than others do. Again the pitfall with the private and social insurance schemes is that it covers only a very small portion of health care cost. The poor either resort to private sector by incurring loans or get no care at all.

A recent study on health care seeking behaviour of Kalanjiam Foundation members has shown "over-use of private care even for minor ailments at twice the cost compared to at government facility. Over-use of private care and high-cost of drug seem to be two problems that poor people suffer from".

It often appears in print media that sometimes even to be allowed to see their newborn babies the poor have to pay. The poor therefore sometimes prefer the paid private services to the free public service. Ground level Staff in public health facilities openly say that, since these people are getting free service, they have no right to expect good behaviour. Our system lacks the mechanism to identify and target the poor when the system is meant to provide service to the poor.

There are reports to suggest that approximately over 20 million Indians are pushed below the poverty line every year because of the effect of out of pocket spending on health care. In urban areas, it is the rich class who visit hospitals. Most of the employed classes enjoy the medical expenses reimbursement benefits. Senior citizens either have the backing of the financial savings or are under the coverage of insurance. Therefore private sectors that attract such “well-to-do” patients continuously plough in resources. Consequently the health care facilities are continuously upgraded in the private healthcare sector. This is a constant cycle, where only the affluent classes reap the benefits.

The inequality between rural and urban health has been augmented due to increased activity of the private healthcare sector. This has resulted in increased number of health care services available at the urban levels and reduced access to quality medical care in the rural areas.

The recent phenomenon of economic liberalization was expected to bring about access and affordability of health care along with other social welfare sectors with decentralized economic units. These reforms were intended to have many far-reaching implications for access to health coverage. But studies show that they have brought about a number of harmful effects by marginalizing the poor and pushing the cost of health care treatment further up. While insurance can be an insulating factor against the financial damage in times of sickness, continued reliance on the employment system to pay the premium to health insurance potentially make the system unviable for the poor.

HEALTH PROMOTION MODELS ADOPTED IN DIFFERENT COUNTRIES

A number of steps have been taken by government agencies of both underdeveloped and developed countries in the last decade to make the health service model more effective. In order to deliver a better service a number of theories and models that underpin the practice of health promotion are designed.

There have been quite a few notable health promotion models by Government policy makers of the US, United Kingdom, Northern Ireland, Australia etc.

The US

The following information has been adapted from the "US Department of Health and Human Services"(2005).

A health promotion model was based on the following principles in 2005.

- An integrated set of propositions that serve as an explanation for a phenomenon.
- Introduced after a phenomenon has already revealed a systematic set of uniformities.
- A systematic arrangement of fundamental principles that provide a basis for explaining certain happenings of life

The Models are as follows:

- A subclass of a theory. It provides a plan for investigating and or addressing a phenomenon
- Does not attempt to explain the processes underlying learning, but only to represent them
- Provides the vehicle for applying the theories

United Kingdom

The National Health Service (NHS) in United Kingdom (UK) provides the majority of healthcare in the nation, from general practitioners to accident and emergency care, long-term healthcare, and dentistry, while the actual delivery of healthcare is implemented through a mix of public and private sector providers. But the Government will not involve private providers to simply replace the shortcomings of the government hospitals. This will not happen if the incentives of all providers are aligned with desirable outcomes. This is the health care model United Kingdom has developed to take care of its citizens.

The role of hospitals is to support community-based care services in promoting health and wellbeing. An effective hospital system will always be required but in an integrated system the most expensive component – hospital services – must be used as efficiently as possible. It is of primary importance that we adopt a whole systems approach to ensure that we get the right balance of investment in services both in the acute sector and in the primary and community sectors. It is also important that we work together through innovative ways of working to share good practice and share resources to the benefit of the patient. Overall, we will implement the integrated programme of investment and reconfiguration set out in Developing Better Services. Within each Board area, the Area Programme Board has responsibility for taking forward the developments under Developing Better Services.

Northern Ireland

The alliances for health programme works to meet this challenge through:

- Policy development and advice;
- Research and evaluation;
- Public and professional information;
- Training and professional development

The workplace is a setting where many people spend the largest proportion of their time. Therefore, employers can play a key role in contributing to the health of their employees and in turn the health of their organization. A workplace where the health and well being of employees is a priority can help improve health and reduce health inequalities.

The health of the workforce both physical and psychological is a major contributor to the success or otherwise of an organization, and can enhance organizational performance and help organizations to gain a competitive advantage.

Organizations implementing workplace health programmes can realize the following benefits:

Some of the actions contained in these health plans include:

- ❖ Developing management practices and policies, which support health;
- ❖ Providing opportunities and activities to promote health and well being;
- ❖ Implementing improvements to the workplace, which protect the safety and health of employees and promote a positive working environment. The learning from the initiative has resulted in the following outcomes:

A healthy workplace 'model' that small businesses can use to develop their own healthy workplace programmes. This includes three key themes, seven quality criteria and a self-evaluation framework.

A user-friendly programme needs assessment process that results in a tailored health action plan, which meets the needs of the individual organization and its employees. The Health Promotion Agency is committed to supporting the continuing training and professional development needs of all those involved in promoting health in Northern Ireland. To do this it provides a high quality programme made up of a series of training events as well as a comprehensive support service for the development and delivery of training and education in health promotion.

The events are open to people working to promote health and fees are subsidized by the Agency. The training features a range of events including workshops, seminars and conferences. A variety of methods are used to create learning opportunities. These include interactive group work, tutorials and reflective practice. The Agency works in partnership with other organizations to assess need and ensure training events are planned, delivered and evaluated to meet those needs.

Australia

The Australian Government program's integrated service access models support efficient, effective and consistent consumer access to services. They also reflect individual organization characteristics and local circumstances, and further embed community health within the service system. This resource guide has been developed to assist Community Health Service (CHS) managers to review, select, implement and evaluate service access models. It outlines the importance of service access models in supporting Service Coordination and provides a summary of the context.

It identifies various service access models and describes and compares benefits and challenges associated with each. Factors influencing the selection of a service access model and the desirable outcomes an effective service access system can support are articulated. It includes implementation and change management strategies, as well as evaluation methodologies. Counseling Services in Community Health Services (CHSs) aim to improve well being in the community by offering supportive counseling, therapy, practical support, advocacy and referral and linkage to other services as needed.

Services can be provided on a one-to-one basis and in groups to adults, adolescents, children and families. The aim is to ensure that all Victorians have access to affordable, effective counseling that is physically accessible, and culturally appropriate. CHS Counseling Services can assist with a wide range of issues, for example family and relationship issues, coping with chronic illness, depression, anxiety and related conditions.

Expenditure on CHS Counseling Services in 2005-06 was approximately $16 million. In addition, many CHSs receive funding from other Department of Human Services or Australian Government programs to provide specialized counseling including alcohol and other drugs, gambling, financial counseling, family support, and family violence. Some specialist mental health services are co-located with CHSs. All of these arrangements support better integration and coordination of counseling services at a local level. In 2004-05, CHS Counseling Services provided 248,667 services to approximately 48,200 people. The most common problems were depression, anxiety and family and relationship difficulties.

Quality improvement

Recognizing the burden of common mental health and social problems, such as depression and anxiety, the Victorian Government committed an additional $10.6 million over 3 years from 2000, to a program of service expansion and improvement of CHS Counseling Services. Services were expanded and a review of counseling services in CHS's was conducted which guided a number of service quality improvements.

Review of counseling services in community health services-

The Review committee proposed initiatives to improve the specification and quality of Counseling Services in CHS's and was conducted in two stages.

Stage One

The findings of the review are explained in the Stage One report Review of Counseling Services in Community Health Discussion Paper 2002. This report also outlined emerging themes and policy directions for Community Health Program funded counseling services.

As a result of the findings from Stage One a number of initiatives were undertaken including:

- Projects to increase access and quality of counseling provided in rural areas,
- Counseling services in each region received additional funding for expansion
- Minor works grants were provided to improve the physical infrastructure of counseling facilities in CHS's.

Leadership initiatives were conducted in all regions to sustain improved practices in counseling services by building local networks to discuss 'best practices'.

Foundations for primary care mental- health treatment services in Victoria 2004, was laid to improve coordination and collaboration between state and Commonwealth departments with responsibility for primary mental health initiatives.

Stage Two

Stage two of the review focused on planning for the future, producing a public consultation draft, Counseling in Community Health Services: Future directions and guidelines for quality counseling'. 'Future Directions' also includes draft guidelines that were developed after extensive consultation with stakeholders.

Public consultations were held between March and July 2005. Thirty-eight submissions were also received from Community Health Services, General Practice Divisions, Mental Health Services, Alcohol & Drug Services.

Those agencies and networks that provided written feedback were invited to a series of focus groups that were held in November 2005 to explore the main themes in the feedback. The focus groups were well attended, with representatives from Community Health Services, Mental Health Services, General Practice Divisions and registration boards. The outcomes from the consultations, written submissions and focus groups will inform the development of the final version of the policy paper.

A submission process was held in late 2005 to select ten Community Health Services to demonstrate implementation of the five key guidelines.

There were 36 submissions in total, 24 from rural regions and 12 from metropolitan regions. Due to the high level of enthusiasm demonstrated in the submissions from rural areas, five additional rural project proposals received funding. These projects proposed innovative service development consistent with Future Directions in regional and rural settings.

Given below is a list of participating services. A range of current or new initiatives were guided by the directions outlined in 'Future Directions', as follows:

- **Regional Community Health Counselor's forums**

During 2005-06 each of the eight Department of Human Services Regions selected a Community Health Service to host three regional forums each year for Community Health (CH) Counselors.

The forums were theme based, for example, depression or working with families, and typically theme included a knowledgeable guest speaker; time to work - out the theme of the day, presentations, participating in services and discussion time.

The forums provided an opportunity for services to showcase research and innovative approaches to service delivery and enable networking between counselors.

The forums aim to support the implementation and sustainability of service improvements throughout each region and encourage enthusiastic, innovative approaches to counseling.

- **Single Session Work project**

The Counseling Review recommended training in Single Session Work (SSW) for Community Health Counselors. Single Session Work is an evidence-based approach that increases responsiveness to client needs and assists services to manage demand. Single Session Work promotes making the most of the first contact, whilst setting up options for further work if necessary.

During 2004-05 training in Single Session Work was offered to Community Health Counselors in rural and metropolitan locations throughout Victoria.

The project was extended to include implementation support to Community Health Services wishing to incorporate SSW into their counseling services and SSW training for Alcohol and Drug Workers and Problem Gambling Counselors based in CHSs.

The project also includes an action research component. An action research framework would be developed to collate and analyze collected data.

The research framework would guide CHSs to monitor actively and map changes in their counseling services resulting from SSW. CHSs would collect pre and post implementation data to inform changes to waiting lists client throughout, and the number of sessions attended by clients.

- **Family therapy skills training for community health counselors**

Family therapy skills training was offered to CH Counselors during 2006. The training was held in regional and metropolitan locations throughout Victoria. The training was aimed at providing CH Counselors with strategies to increase effectiveness in working with families.

➢ **Clinical Supervision training**

Training in Clinical Supervision was offered during 2006 to senior experienced CH Counselors. This project did include consultation with CHS management and counselors about their views and preferences with regard to the provision of clinical supervision. The purpose of this project was to support the provision of high quality effective counseling in Community Health Services.

➢ **Developing Better Services**

A model of health care which would provide high quality safe services which are accessible for all and provided by well trained, motivated staff in modern settings.

The overarching model by Gelberg L et al (1997) for future health care services shall be set out in the stratagy, expanding the behavioral model of health services to explore the health status and health services use of homeless and other vulnerable populations".

Chart -3.3

The Model For Future Health Care Services

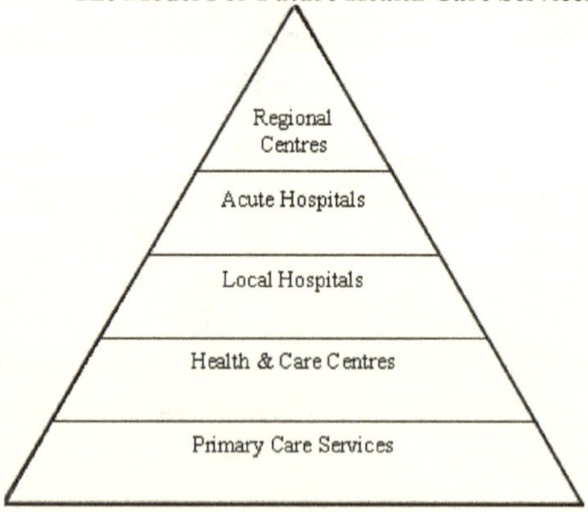

Model by Gelberg L et al (1997)

According to integrated service access model, over the next twenty years two distinct forces will define the shape of health services, namely:

Greater provision of generalist services within communities or on a day-patient or out-patient basis than the case at present. These will include primary care services, chronic disease management, social services maintaining and enhancing independence, and much of the surgery currently provided on an inpatient basis.

Greater specialisation particularly within acute hospital services. This will promote the quality of services by ensuring that professionals deal with a 'critical mass' of similar cases to achieve sufficient expertise. New specialised medical technologies and techniques will keep more people alive who would otherwise die through illness or trauma.

Health promotion measures in India

National Planning Commission (MOHFW Statistics, 1998) identified following strategic themes, which must be simultaneously pursued in "stand alone", or inter-sectoral programmes in order to achieve the national socio-demographic goals for 2010. These are presented below:

A starting point, for a possible model, is the comprehensive package of healthcare recommended by the National Commission of Macroeconomics and Health (NCMH), with a standardized schedule of benefits at an estimated liability of Rs. 1,160 per capita, per annum. The current per capita cost of this schedule of benefits (in all permutations and combinations) should not exceed $40 per capita, per annum.

State governments will identify the target population to be covered, so that its commitment does not exceed its resources. Public funding in healthcare is already directed towards below the poverty line segments, but resources permitting, state governments could consider the inclusion of above poverty line segments.

In this model, the state government would determine the eligibility criteria for identifying service providers. An independent panel would invite applications and empanel all candidate providers, public, private, not-for-profit NGOs, who meet these criteria

❖ **Decentralized Planning and Programme Implementation**

The 73rd and 74th Constitutional Amendments Act, 1992, made health, family welfare and education a responsibility of village panchayats. The panchayati raj institutions are an important means of furthering decentralized planning and programme implementation in the context of the NPP 2000. However, in order to realize their potential, they need strengthening by further delegation of administrative and financial powers, including powers of resource mobilization.

Further, since 33 percent of elected panchayat seats are reserved for women, representative committees of the panchayats (headed by an elected woman panchayat member) should be formed to promote a gender sensitive, multi-sectoral agenda for population stabilization that will "think, plan and act locally, and support nationally".

These committees may identify area specific unmet needs for reproductive health services, and prepare need-based, demand driven, socio-demographic plans at the village level, aimed at identifying and providing responsive, people-centered and integrated, basic reproductive and child health care.

Panchayats demonstrating exemplary performance in the compulsory registration of births, deaths, marriages, and pregnancies, universalizing the small family norm, increasing safe deliveries, bringing about reductions in infant and maternal mortality, and promoting compulsory education up to age 14, will be nationally recognized and honored.

❖ **Convergence of Service Delivery at Village Levels**

Efforts at population stabilization will be effective only if we direct an integrated package of essential services at village and household levels. Below district levels, current health infrastructure includes 2,500 community health centres, 25,000 primary health centres (each covering a population of 30,000), and 1.36 lakh sub centres (each covering a population of 5,000 in the plains and 3,000 in hilly regions).

Inadequacies in the existing health infrastructure have led to an unmet need of 28 percent for contraception services and obvious gaps in coverage and outreach.

Health care centres are over-burdened and struggle to provide services with limited personnel and equipment. Absence of supportive supervision, lack of training in inter-personal communication, and lack of motivation to work in rural areas, together impede citizens' access to reproductive and child health services, and contribute to poor quality of services and an apparent insensitivity to client's needs.

The last 50 years have demonstrated the unsuitability of these yardsticks for provision of health care infrastructure, particularly for remote, inaccessible, or sparsely populated regions in the country like hilly and forested areas, desert regions and tribal areas. We need to promote a more flexible approach, by extending basic reproductive and child health care through mobile clinics and counseling services.

Further, recognizing that government alone cannot make up for the inadequacies in health care infrastructure and services, in order to resolve unmet needs and extend coverage, the involvement of the voluntary sector and the non-government sector in partnership with the government is essential.

- **Tribal Communities, Hill Area Populations and Displaced and Migrant Populations**

In general, populations in remote and low-density areas do not have adequate access to affordable health care services. Tribal populations often have high levels of morbidity arising from poor nutrition, particularly in situations where they are involuntarily displaced or resettled. Frequently, they have low levels of literacy, coupled with high infant, child, and maternal mortality.

They remain under-served in the coverage of reproductive and child health services. These communities need special attention in terms of basic health, and reproductive and child health services. The special needs of tribal groups, which need to be addressed, include the provision of mobile clinics that will be responsive to seasonal variations in the availability of work and income. Information and counseling on infertility, and regular supply of standardized medication will be included.

Information, education and communication (IEC) of family welfare messages must be clear, focused and disseminated everywhere, including the remote corners of the country, and in local dialects. This will ensure that the messages are effectively conveyed. These need to be strengthened and their outreach widened, with locally relevant, and locally comprehensible media and messages. On the model of the total literacy campaigns which have successfully mobilized local populations, there is need to undertake a massive national campaign on population related issues, via artists, popular film stars, doctors, vaidyas, hakims, nurses, local midwives, women's organizations, and youth organizations.

In this backdrop it would be pertinent to study the innovations in healthcare in the US. Hospital Corporation of America successfully pioneered a model innovation that allowed it to consolidate the management of dozens of facilities and thereby realize economies of scale unknown in the fragmented health care industry. The national chain – currently 190 hospitals and 200 outpatient centers - succeeded in part because it did not try to compete head to head with politically powerful academic medical centers. Instead it grew mostly through expansion into underprivileged communities, where customers were grateful for a local hospital and where doctors welcomed the chance to work. Although in 1990 it weathered the crisis of misdeeds, with new management it continues to perform well.

According to the Journal of the American Medical Association, September 8, 2004 Switzerland's excellent healthcare system costs only 11 percent of GDP, verses 16 percent of the United States.

Views of Important personalities on health promotion

Former President A.P.J. Abdul Kalam emphasized the need for providing urban amenities in rural areas in our country while speaking to the nation on the eve of the 56th republic days on 26-Jan-2005 (A.P.J. Abdul Kalam).

Macarov (1982) has remarked that a renewed concern for work satisfaction has its origins in two perspectives:

- Traditional assumption that a dissatisfied worker is a less productive one.
- A broad public interest in satisfying work.

These factors have sparked a renewed emphasis on human relations in the work place in the form of quality of work life programmes (Chelte et al 1989).

When Evo Morales was elected as president of Bolivia the entire Latin American countries in the hemisphere congratulated him because he came from an indigenous background. He was hailed as a greatest hero as he represents his country's indigenous population in the United Nations. Perhaps it would be necessary to applaud him because he worked with indigenous groups for almost 30 long years, educating them on their right to education, health and sustainable wage for living. The quotation given below aptly summarizes the need for improvement in health care delivery in Tribal areas (Front line Magazine Mar 14, 2008).

"Indigenous people are amongst the poorest and most marginalized population groups experiencing extreme levels of health deprivation" (Nettleton C 2004).

The Magsaysay award winner and distinguished doctor Dr. Sudarshan representing the Tribal populations of B.R.Hills, Karnataka, India, has vehemently expressed that both the central and the state Governments have neglected the indigenous health care system for the Tribals. Consequently he is of the opinion that all health care of the Tribals must be addressed with large outlays in both state and central budget. The quotation below justifies the statement.

"Improving indigenous health as well as eliminating the indigenous/non-indigenous health divide requires addressing the knowledge gap related to understanding the patterns of indigenous health deprivation" (Clark S 2005).

Limited studies are available on infant mortality and hardly any study is available on maternal mortality among the tribal population (Basu, 1992).

In the light of the current situation "Insurance" is probably one of the cost effective, systematic risk transfer management mechanism.

Insurance

The original blue print for health care in India through Hospitals and Primary Health Centers in different locations is planned well with the idea of covering all the citizens and taking care of all their health needs. But, in comparison to developed countries, per capita insurance is low in India and India's insurance penetration is as low as 1.95 percent of the population, which ranks 51 in the world.

Community health insurance (CHI) is slowly gaining momentum in India. A number of agencies have put in place schemes for providing health security to the poor. Models of such insurance schemes include SEWA, Ahmedabad, Yashasvini Health Scheme launched by Narayana Hrudayalaya, Bangalore, the central Government's Universal Health Insurance Scheme, and Arogya Raksha Yojana launched by Biocon and Narayana Hrudayalaya, Bangalore.

Article 41 of Indian constitution makes a provision for social security and insurance in case of sickness and disablement. Medical claim or med-claim policy recently has been improved. To overcome operational inconvenience all the sub heading have been regrouped and offer a re-imbursement of medical expenses to help the insurer towards any illness, injury, disease contracted during the period of insurance coverage.

Even among the educated and medically insured, the knowledge about insurance benefits is poor. A study conducted by Dr R. Vasanth Gopal and Mathew Jose K in Kerala on 300 insured persons, only 18 percent were fully aware, 22 percent were not at all aware and remaining 60 percent were partially aware of the formalities of claiming the benefits. Further studies reveal that 87 percent of the insured persons have not availed of the disablement benefits.

According to census 2001, Kerala achieved literacy rate of 90.92 percent compared to all India rate of 65.38 percent. Kerala being the most literate state and not being able to achieve the heath care delivery, one can surmise the situation in the illiterate tribal areas in our country (Census 2001).

Health insurance "YASHASWINI "first phase was introduced in Karnataka in 2003. Second phase of YASHASWINI was introduced on 1st June 2004 with the idea of penetrating into the rural market. Selected hospitals and nursing homes in towns and district headquarters are earmarked to provide the health care services under this scheme. But not all the poor could get the benefits of the scheme. Some of the limiting factors of the scheme are

- Member ship validity for one year only
- A few taluk level private hospitals without adequate facilities considered.

Relying on private health insurance is likely to play some role in the short term, since the insurance market has been liberalized, and this consumes little additional public resources. The lack of an effective public health system has led to a booming private system. Growing middle class in the 1990s has led to the emergence of the private medical sector in India, which is increasingly being commercialized.

Three years after a community health insurance scheme was implemented by the government of Karnataka and Karuna Trust around 200,000 poor people have benefited, paying annual premiums of just Rs. 30 per year for insurance cover of Rs 50 per day of hospitalisation (Bharathi Ghanashyam).

As a result, for example, overall health insurance coverage is low in India (Gumber 2002). Estimates suggest that less than 10% of people in India have access to health insurance, and a majority of them belong to the organized sector (Gumber 1998, Ellis et al 2000). This suggests that for people in rural and interior areas there is a need to provide health care service urgently. All tribals fall under the top priority.

Improper health care system delivery leads to self-medication, which is another possibility, resulting in incorrect self-diagnosis and inappropriate dosage thereby inducing the side effects (Chang and Trivedi 2003).

A recent study by Gumber and Kulkarni (2000) suggests that the rural respondents in Gujarat were willing to pay an annual premium of Rs. 80 and Rs. 95 for coverage for hospitalization, chronic ailment, and specialist consultation and an additional 16% if there was coverage of transport costs, medicine costs and diagnostic charges.

However, they are poor, most of them are not in employer-employee relationships, they do not have any form of insurance or security (e.g.maternity benefits, retirement, health insurance), nor do they have representative organizations that might help them fight for these benefits (Ahmad et al. 1991). The Government of India has designed a number of schemes to address this overarching health threat. One of the most fascinating programmes has been National Rural Health Mission.

National Rural Health Mission (NRHM)

National Rural Health Mission (NRHM) provides a broad conceptual framework about the health care programme earmarked for rural poor. NRHM is not a new programme of the Govt. of India but NRHM is a combination of national programmes, namely, the Reproductive and Child Health II project, (RCH II) the National Disease Control Programmes (NDCP) and the Integrated Disease Surveillance Project (IDSP). NRHM will also enable Ayurveda, Yoga, Unani, Siddha and Homeopathy Systems of Health (AYUSH) to become part of the main stream.

It covers the entire country, with special focus on 18 states where the challenge of strengthening poor public health systems and thereby improving key health indicators is the greatest. These are Uttar Pradesh, Uttaranchal, Madhya Pradesh, Chhattisgarh, Bihar, Jharkhand, Orissa, Rajasthan, Himachal Pradesh, Jammu and Kashmir, Assam, Arunachal Pradesh, Manipur, Meghalaya, Nagaland, Mizoram, Sikkim and Tripura.

While providing a broad framework for operationalization, NRHM lists a set of core and supplementary strategies to meet its goals.

The core strategy of NRHM will include decentralization of villages and district level Rural Planning and Management and to appoint ASHA to create awareness, to counsel women and to mobilize community facilities for accessing health related services. ASHA is expected to escort pregnant women for delivery to institutions as PHC/FRU.

The Ayurvedic system will improve management capacity to organize health system and Public Heath Services.

Supplementary Strategies include regulation of the private sector to improve equity and reduce out of pocket expenses, foster public–private partnerships to meet national public health goals, re-orienting medical education, introduction of effective risk pooling mechanisms and social insurance to raise the health security of the poor, and taking full advantage of local health traditions.

At the State level, the Chief Minister shall lead the State Health Mission. It shall be co-chaired by the Health Minister with the State Health Secretary, as convenient, and with representation from related Departments, NGOs, private professionals etc.

The District Health Mission shall be led by the Chairman, Zilla Parishad, and be convened by the District Head of the Health Department. It shall have representation from all relevant Departments, NGOs and private professionals.

- **Role of the State Governments under the NRHM**

The mission covers the entire country. The 18 high focus states are Uttar Pradesh, Uttaranchal, Madhya Pradesh, Chhattisgarh, Bihar, Jharkhand, Orissa, Rajasthan, Himachal Pradesh, Jammu and Kashmir, Assam, Arunachal Pradesh, Manipur, Meghalaya, Nagaland, Mizoram, Sikkim and Tripura.The rest of the states have to follow the pattern of high focus states for programme management units and upgradation of SC, PHC and CHC through integrated financial envelope.

NRHM provides board conceptual framework. The states would project operational modalities in their State Action Plans, to be decided in consultation with the Mission Steering Group. NRHM would prioritize funding for addressing inter-state and intra-district disparities in terms of health infrastructure and indicators.

The states would sign a Memorandum of Understanding with the Government of India, indicating their commitment of increasing contribution to Public Health Budget (preferably by 10% each year), increased devolution to Panchayati Raj Institutions as per 73rd Constitution (Amendment) Act, and performance benchmarks for release of funds.

- **Roles of the State and District Health Missions**

The State Health Mission shall prepare the roadmap for architectural correction of the Health System, including merger/integration of vertical structures; delegation and decentralization of administrative and financial powers; empowering the Panchayati Raj Institutions (PRIs); preparation of Operational Guidelines for the implementation of the Mission; logistics arrangements; disease surveillance whereas, the District Health Mission shall control, guide and manage all public health institutions in the district and at sub-district levels. It will be responsible for preparation and implementation of an integrated District Action Plan in respect of funds received from all funding agencies into the District Health Fund.

- **Flexibilities available to the States under the NRHM**

The States shall have flexibility to project operational modalities in their State Action Plans, which would be decided in consultation with the Mission Steering Group.

The NRHM is being launched as a framework of partnership among Government of India, related Departments of the Government, especially Departments of Women & Child Development, Drinking Water Supply, Panchayati Raj, and Development of North Eastern Region, State Governments, Panchayat Raj Institutions, NGOs, and private health providers. The detailing of strategies would continue during the Mission with the combined effort of all the stakeholders.

Outlay of NRHM

The Outlay of the NRHM for 2005-06 was Rs. 6713 crores. The Outlay of the Mission in subsequent years did dependent on the Outlay of the Ministry of Health and Family Welfare.

The Budget Outlay of the Ministry of Health and Family Welfare has increased by 30% in 2005-06 over the previous financial year. The States would prepare comprehensive Action Plans for NRHM, indicating priorities for funding, which shall be covered under the increased Outlays expected in the coming years.

- **State contribution in term of funds under the NRHM**

  The States are required to sign MoU with the Govt. of India, committing a minimal increase of 10% for Public Health expenditure in the State Budget each year.

- **Fund flow mechanism**

  The States will be given in advance, an indication of funds to be devolved. State Action Plan would be prepared, which would be funded through a financial envelope for RCH-II and funding under NDCP. The Societies for Health and Family Welfare programmes would be merged into one integrated Society at State and District level to enable "funneling" of funds. The NRHM Budget Head would retain Sub-Budget Heads for the erstwhile Societies.

- **Role of Panchayati Raj Institutions (PRI) in the NRHM**

  For developing the Village Health Plan with the support of the ANM, ASHA, AWW and Self Help Groups, Block Level Panchayat Samitis will co-ordinate the work of the GP in their jurisdiction and will serve as a link to the DHM. The major role of Panchayat is to select ASHA preferably from their village.

- **Reasons to form Programme management units**

  To help in better management of health services in relation to monitoring and implementation of programme with the help of professionally qualified managers, viz., financial personnel and data managers at state and district level.

The states are expected to review the state level performance in at least 4 districts on half yearly basis. Where as the role of primary medical unit (PMU) at district level is to ensure regular and continuous provision of MCH services, including out reach services as scheduled, to strengthen critical interventions and ensure continuous availability of supplies and equipment from the state HQ to the service provider to trained manpower with appropriate skills, to facilitate improvement in context of quality and coverage of services, to ensure adequate and efficient utilization of funds, to monitor the performance of MCH services.

Infrastructure available with AYUSH under NRHM are:

- The personnel of AYUSH may work under the same roof as health infrastructure.
- The posting of any one Doctor of AYUSH System.
- Provision of one specialist of any of AYUSH System as per the local need in CHC.
- AYUSH dispensary, which is not doing well, may be merged with PHC/CHC.
- Cross referral between Allopathic & AYUSH stream should be encouraged based on the need for the same.
- AYUSH Doctors should be involved in IEC health promotion and also supervisory activities.

Key activities in the Year 2005-2006

Broadly speaking, the common activities under NRHM, which are uniformly applicable across all States/UTs over and above those proposed under ongoing programmes like RCH and National Disease Control Programmes, are as follows:

- Constitution of State and District Health Missions
- Merger of Health and Family Welfare Societies
- Preparation of State Action Plan, which identifies sectoral needs and priorities
- Finalizing performance benchmarks for MoU
- Signing of MOU between State and GOI
- Preparation of District Action Plans.
- Upgrading two CHCs in every district to the level of Indian Public Health Standards, including the provision for two rooms in these CHCs for bringing AYUSH practitioners under the same roof.
- Formation of Rogi Kalyan Samitis

- Immunization strengthening through induction of Auto Disabled Syringes and arrangement for alternate vaccine delivery at immunization sites.
- Organizing mobile medical services at district level.
- Organizing Health Camp at AWW level on a fixed day in a month for assured services for women and child health care.
- Provision of household toilets.
- Strengthening institutional delivery under Janani Suraksha Yojana (JSY) through provision of escort and referral services by ASHA & subsidized hospital services for BPL women.
- Establishing systems to increase accountability of health systems to PRIs.
- Selection and training of ASHA, including provision of drug kits
- Organizing Health Melas as a platform to inform and educate the public on NRHM
- Provision of generic drugs, both AYUSH and allopathic, at village, SC/PHC/CHC level, for common ailments.

Some activities as mentioned above shall be specially funded in the 18 high focus States.

Additional inputs: States were expected to receive Rs. 20 lakhs/CHC to two CHCs in every district for bringing them on par with IPHS.

- Maintenance grant of Rs. 1 lakh per CHC, after constitution of Rogi Kalyan
- Samiti at that level.
- Untied fund of Rs. 10,000 per Sub-centre.
- Supply of additional drugs (allopathic and AYUSH) at Sub-centre and PHC
- Mobile Medical Unit for district
- 50% districts in EAG states to get Rs. 10 lakhs/district for district planning
- Funds for training of ASHAs

The State and District Action Plans were formulated within the first six months. Village Action Plans were formulated during the second year. State Action Plans in Year I would include outlays for RCH II, National Disease Control Programme and the Integrated Disease Surveillance Programme. The State Action Plan would also include funds under AYUSH, Finance Commission grants- in-aid, Rashtriya Sam Vikas Yojana, external bilateral funding, and large NGO grants. Even though budgeting would remain separate for better convergence, the outlays and programmes to improve sanitation, nutrition etc. should also be reflected in the State Action Plan. Once the District Plans are ready, the State Action Plan should be based on those Plans.

For 2005-2006, districts consolidated existing resources within the HFW sector, plan for convergence with nutrition, water and sanitation, and focus on identifying areas in the district with poor indicators and the greatest need of financial resources. After Year 2, detailed District Action Plans, based on Village Health Plans were developed by the DHM.

Project Management cost for all districts is covered under the financial envelope of RCH II. 18 high focus States shall make contractual engagement of skilled professionals.

The institutional arrangement for the NRHM as well as Total Sanitation Campaign are same at District and Village levels. However, budgeting for the two programmes remain separate. Integration with ICDS implies joint planning. Use of AWC as the hub of the NRHM interventions in the village, joint reporting and monitoring on common indicators, and engagement with the AWW are key factors in village planning and implementation.

In the year 2005-2006 there was no separate Budget Head for NRHM. Creation of a new Budget Head for NRHM was from the year 2006. The initial programmes maintained sub-Budget Heads under the omnibus NRHM Budget Head.

There was only one MOU, subsuming the MOU for all programmes integrated under NRHM. Signing of this MoU was the precondition to release of second tranche of funds in October 2005.

Performance benchmarks under NRHM would include performance indicators in respect of all integrated programmes. In addition, NRHM requires the following activities to be completed.

Constitution of State and District Health Missions and Merger of Health and Family Welfare Societies

- **Signing of MOU for NRHM between State and GOI**

The Frequently asked questions (FAQs) are prepared for the website of the institute so that the PG Students and students of Distance Learning Course may have knowledge about the NRHM programme launched by the Govt. of India and to be implemented by the Ministry of Health & Family Welfare in 18 states of the country. These questions & answers are prepared keeping in view the role of NRHM , the apex body attached to the Ministry of Health & Family Welfare to guide in technical matters. These questions & answers are in simple language, which even the staff at the peripheral level in the states can understand easily.

Being the apex body of the Ministry of Health & Family Welfare, the institute can guide the ministry by preparing teaching module for senior level trainers and for refresher training of ASHA workers. The Training of Trainers can also be undertaken by NIHFW, along with developing refresher training curriculum for ASHA workers and other staff associated with this programme.

Monitoring and mid term evaluation of various schemes like JSY, ASHA workers, IPHS are taken up as a regular activity of the institute for a period of 5 years. End term evaluation can be undertaken at the close of the programme.

BRIEF PHARMACEUTICAL HISTORY IN INDIA

Medicine constitutes an integral part of medical treatment. Acharya states, "Improvements in health indicators will require sustained increases in income-earning opportunities in laggard states and substantial improvements in the provision of health services in them." Health care costs continue to rise. "Pharmaceutical costs are increasing faster than any other component of the health care expense" (George Merck in 1952).

"Drugs, a "decisive technology", constitute 20-60% of total health care expenditure in developing countries A major portion of the private health care spending goes to drugs. Per capita private drug spending in India is estimated as US $ 16 (Abel-Smith 1994).

It is imperative that hospitals, drug companies and Government agencies need to formulate the best way to keep health care affordable without adversely affecting access to quality care. Branded drug prescription is a major contributor to cost escalations. With the rising cost of the drugs in view, the Government of India enacted the Indian patent act (IPA) in 1970 in which foreign (MNC) pharma companies could take benefit of the manufacturing process only and not the end product.

Due to inadequate availability of particular brands of drugs with the government stores, urgency (need) pushes patients towards private stores.

Although the Government has made a provision to free distribution of medicine following a prescription of a medical doctor, non-availability in Government hospitals is a concern. Majority of government health care institutions including those in rural areas lack critical inputs such as drugs (Government of India 2002).

As a result patients are forced to go to private drug store. Drug prices act as a strong barrier to seeking effective health care in India, as they are high and people lack the purchasing power. There are instances where people go without drugs (by extension without treatment) or buy a small proportion of the required doses of drugs due to high prices.

"While the share of drugs in private spending is as high as 60-70% depending on the type of illness, their share in government spending is less than 10%" (Varatharajan et al 2002).

Generic drugs offer an important tool for reducing the rate of growth in overall health expenditure. Today drug development is a business decision for a pharmaceutical company. Drug houses, being sales driven, are ultimately responsible to show increase in turnover, higher profits and dividend to share holders. Thus return of investment (ROI) being the nucleus of marketing philosophy, the research driven companies mostly concentrate on the market of diseases of the rich countries to maximize the profits.

It is estimated that of the 1700 odd drugs developed between 1975 and 1998 in the world, only 13 drugs were developed for the poor man's tropical diseases (Mishra et al 2003).

Down the years, business compulsions have forced pharmaceutical companies to go in for integration, take over and mergers. As a result, the number of companies is reduced, giving way to monopoly by some.

Statistics provided by the Director General of Commercial Intelligence and Statistics indicate that the number of drug companies have come down from 252 in 1996-97 to 205 in 2002-03 (DGCI&S 2002-03).

Medicines at times could be a lifetime companion in chronic conditions like high blood pressure, diabetes or arthritis. If afflicted in old age, diminishing purchasing power can be an additional negative dimension. Although, since time immemorial, in our country we have treasured the knowledge of alternative medical systems, its formal recognition and integration was late and did not keep pace with the population explosion.

"Only in the late 1970s did official health policy refer to any form of integration between western-oriented medical personnel and indigenous medical practitioners" (Health care in India 1995).

The situation gets increasingly worse as time progresses, as drug prices grow faster than the national or per capita income in India. By one estimate, drug prices growth could be 3-5 times higher in India compared to general inflation of about 5-6%. Drug cost has a lion's share to contribute to the soaring cost of overall health care. To keep health care affordable without adversely affecting access to quality care is the greatest challenge of our time.

With multinational drug companies dominating the drug market in our country along with their Indian counterparts, one tangible solution could be the Government stepping in to do large scale manufacturing of generics drugs or to give incentives to private drug manufacturers to produce the generic versions with stringent quality tests.

"With prescription drug (branded drug) costs serving as a major contributor to cost escalations, generic drugs offer an important tool for reducing the rate of growth in overall health expenditure"(G Bhaktavatsalam Vol : XIX Number 1: 16-9).

The National Pharmaceutical Pricing Authority (NPPA) was established in 1997 to improve the speed and transparency of the process of fixing of the prices of bulk drugs and formulations. Drugs industry in general display distinct characteristics compared to FMCG or general commodities in terms of the usual demand-supply-market relationship. There are two major Government Agencies responsible for drug regulation and control.

- Food and Drug Administration (FDA)
- Drug Controller of India (DCI)

While most industries reduce the price of the products with the increase in competition, pharmaceutical companies remain insulated from this factor. An example of best selling cough syrups from multinational pharmaceutical companies in our country bare a testimony to it. With a market growth of over 6 percent and over the counter sales (OTC), the price of these cough syrups have increased over three times in last decade. Fake drugs are also not uncommon. Marketing aggression may sometime lead to over prescriptions of drugs. "A study in Satara district of Maharashtra found that irrational prescriptions were more in the private sector than in the government health services" (Phadke et al 1995).

Evolution Of Pharmaceutical Companies in India

Globally, Indian Pharmaceutical industry ranks 4th in terms of volume and 13th in terms of value. Soon after the independence of our country multinational pharmaceutical companies began their marketing activities in India. Most of them were American, British, German and Switzerland pharmaceutical houses. It was a competition-less market and did not suffer a price control for almost a decade and a half after independence in our country.

Till Independence (1947)

Although there was a great need for medicines due to low income levels and underdeveloped supply chain system pharmaceutical companies were almost nonexistent. Post independently, therefore, the government had to pay urgent attention to the problem and pave the way for the pharmaceutical companies to enter.

1947-1970

During this period India suffered from many epidemics. Most anti-infectives had to be imported. In 1954, the first pharmaceutical company was established namely "Hindustan Antibiotic Limited" (HAL). This was followed by "Indian Drugs and Pharmaceuticals Limited" (IDPL) in 1961.This move of the Government averted the need to import important drugs like penicillin and other anti-infective. During this period the Government also invited multinational drug companies, providing them with incentives to set up their manufacturing units in India.

1970-1979

It was increasingly felt that the common man could not afford the medicine due to cost. Therefore, the Government introduced "Drug Price Control Act" (DPCO) with the objective to control the prices of important drugs. This move ushered in the investment and growth of indigenous pharmaceutical companies. Attractive incentives encouraged Indian companies to surge ahead gradually during the period. "Since then, pharmaceuticals have fallen under price regulation in India; a total of 343 drugs– accounting for 85% of the drug market – were under price control in 1979. Profitability allowed on price-controlled drugs ranged from 40 to 75 percent" (Gupta 2002).

1979-1995

The Government made amendments to the existing Drug Price Control Act (DPCO). It reduced the number of drugs under DPCO from 347 to 163. Higher margins were permitted on the production cost. DPCO was again amended in the year 1987 with the number of drugs reduced from 163 to 145. But not all formulations came under price control. Allowed profitability too went up to 150%.

1995-2001

Again the number of drugs under DPCO was reduced from 145 to 74. The same year the Government signed "General Agreement of Tariffs and Trade" (GATT). This was followed by series of changes in the pharma business in India.

2002-2007

In early part of the year 2002, the Government of India framed Pharmaceutical Policy 2002 and announced the criteria for exercising price control on Pharmaceutical products.

By 2002, the share of drugs under price control went further down to 25% or just 32 drugs. Prior to 1995 when the number of drugs under price control was revised downward, the annual price rise of drugs was estimated as 10-50% (Rare 1999).

It would be higher now under price decontrol. Price decontrol seems to have facilitated the growth of Indian Pharmaceutical industry; it registered a growth of 10% between 1996-97 and 2002-03 (CMIE 2004).

Sales have gone up by 88.8% from Rs. 161.50 billion in 1996-97 to Rs. 304.80 billion in 2002-03. It would be higher now under price decontrol. Price decontrol seems to have facilitated the growth of Indian Pharmaceutical industry; it registered a growth of 10% between 1996-97 and 2002-03 (CMIE 2004).

Pharmaceutical companies indulge in aggressive marketing to sell their products. Selling (advertising) costs represent about 15% of the total revenue indicating that obviously, the burden is passed on to the drug buyers.

Way forward

Generic drugs are a cost effective alternative. It may be noted that the American Medical Association, the largest organization of medical doctors in the USA, has stated that generic drug products are acceptable for use by the American public.

Most hospitals in America routinely use generic drugs for treatment of their patients. Not only are generic drugs cost effective but also they are safe. Generic drugs are bioequivalent (Equal in potency in human body) to their brand name twins. As generics tend to be older, they are generally less risky than new drug therapies. (G Bhaktavatsalam Vol : XIX Number 1: 16-9).

Generic drugs offer sound treatment options for patients. Cost of drugs is high due to research, production cost and high mark-up of the retail prices due to limited competition. Large-scale production of generic drugs can be a practical option to provide economical treatment. Most of the drugs are discovered abroad and are marketed in India only after the patent expiry, which means drug firms would have recovered their research expenses but continue to sell at higher prices. The unique feature of the drug industry is that drugs manufactured by non-research firms are perceived to be less effective and safe. But research confirms in our country that this perception is unfounded. This vicious cycle makes the drugs dearer for patients in rural areas.

Only 21 percent of Americans believe Big Pharmaceutical companies do a good job of serving its customers, down from 60 percent a decade ago, according to a recent Harris Poll (World of Marketing.com 2007).

The Government may also impose compulsory licensing so as to make available the much-needed generic drugs. It is seen that many countries do not have the technological capability for manufacturing and supplying generic drugs even if the laws of those countries permit them to do so.

A PROFILE OF STUDY AREA

The tribal groups inhabit widely varying ecological and geo-climatic conditions (hilly, forest, desert, coastal regions, etc.) in different concentrations throughout the country and are distinct biological isolates with characteristic cultural and socio-economic background. Census 1991 recorded the population of tribal as 67.76 million excluding Jammu & Kashmir (Status of Tribal Women in India").

The tribal population of the country, as per the 2001 census, was 8.43 crore, constituting 8.2% of the total population. The population of tribes had grown at the growth rate of 24.45% during the period 1991-2001 (Ministry of Tribal Affairs 2006-07).

KARNATAKA

Tribal populations in Karnataka are mainly distributed in Districts of Mysore, Chamarajanagar, Chikmagalur, Udupi, and Uttar Kannada. In Karnataka there are about 49 Tribes. They live in remote, inaccessible areas. They constitute about 3.46 million (5.6 Percent) of total population of 52.85 million in Karnataka.

Following are the dominant tribes in Karnataka

Jenu Kurubas : The Jenu Kurubas are primarily a hunter-gatherer tribe, who earned their name from the fact that they are expert honey gatherers. 'Jenu' in their language means 'honey'.

Betta Kurubas: Also a food-gatherer tribe. The Betta Kuruba people specialise in crafting bamboo utensils.

Yeravas: Also a food-gathering tribe. They practice sustenance agriculture. Fishing is their specialty.

Soligas : Soligas too are food gatherers, diversified into marginal agriculture and herding goats.

Table - 4.1: The Tribal population growth in Karnataka in different districts between 1991 to 2001

Bagalkot	261.6%	1991-2001
Dharwad	201.1%	1991-2001
Belgaum	193%	1991-2001
Dakshin Kannada	(2.9)%	1991-2001
Raichur	18.1%	1991-2001
Bellary	18%	1991-2001
Chitradurga	17.5%	1991-2001
Mysore	328%	1991-2001

The Tribal population in Karnataka was 19.16 lakh in 1991 and grew to 34.64 lakh in 2001.The growth is around 80.8 percent. But this increase in population is not by fertility and health care but by addition of several new tribes to the scheduled tribes category (Sridhar Naidu 2001).

Table – 4.2 : The Tribal population growth in Karnataka compared to all India

Tribal Population	Year	Total in lakh	Growth %
All India	1991	8463	
All India	2001	10270.2	21.34
Tribals in Karnataka	1991	19.16	
Tribals in Karnataka	2001	34.64	80.8

(Source : Census of India)

After their traditional rights of access to the forests and its resources were severely curtailed subsequent to the declaration of the national park, the indigenous people have lost their independent livelihood and have been forced to delve into the displaced environment. In the process they have been absorbed as cheap and exploitable daily wagers in the nearby coffee estates. Some of them are employed by the forest dept for the upkeep of the forest. However, this employment is seasonal.

Present study is conducted from districts of Mysore, Kodagu and the coastal district of Uttar Kannada in Karnataka. Tribals from Taluks of H.D. Kote (Mysore), Virajpet (Kodagu) and Kumta (Uttar Kannada) were enrolled in the study. Marked areas in map were the areas under study.

Table- 4.3 : Details of Tribal area under study

District	H.Q.	Area in Sq. KM	Tribal Population	State
Mysore	Mysore	6,269	2624911	Karnataka
Kodagu	Madikeri	4,102	545322	Karnataka
Uttar Kannada	Karawar	10,291	1353299	Karnataka

MYSORE

A total of about 32,000 indigenous people reside in and around Mysore Dist (national park) spread over three Taluks of H D Kote & Hunsur (Mysore Dist) To the Southeast, it borders the Bandipur wildlife sanctuary & Madhumalai sanctuary of Tamil Nadu and the 'Wayanad' wildlife sanctuary of Kerala in the South West. To the West it is separated from the 'Brahmagiri' wildlife sanctuary by coffee plantations The number of Haadis (hamlets) are 138 of which 58 are in the national park. Of the 58 in the park, 33 are in Virajpet Taluk - 22 in H D Kote - 3 in Hunsur. The resident tribes are the Jenu Kurubas, Betta Kurubas, Yeravas, Soligas & sub-castes of the Yeravas (i.e., the Panjeri Yeravas & the Pani Yeravas).

A study conducted by NGO's in Mysore focusing on education conducted a survey under "Back to Basics" programme. The study revealed that less than 3 percent tribal students were able to read and write, 25 percent knew to add in arithmetic, only 18 percent students could divide and 11 percent of them were able to multiply among 656 tribal students.

Map – 4.1 : Map of Mysore District

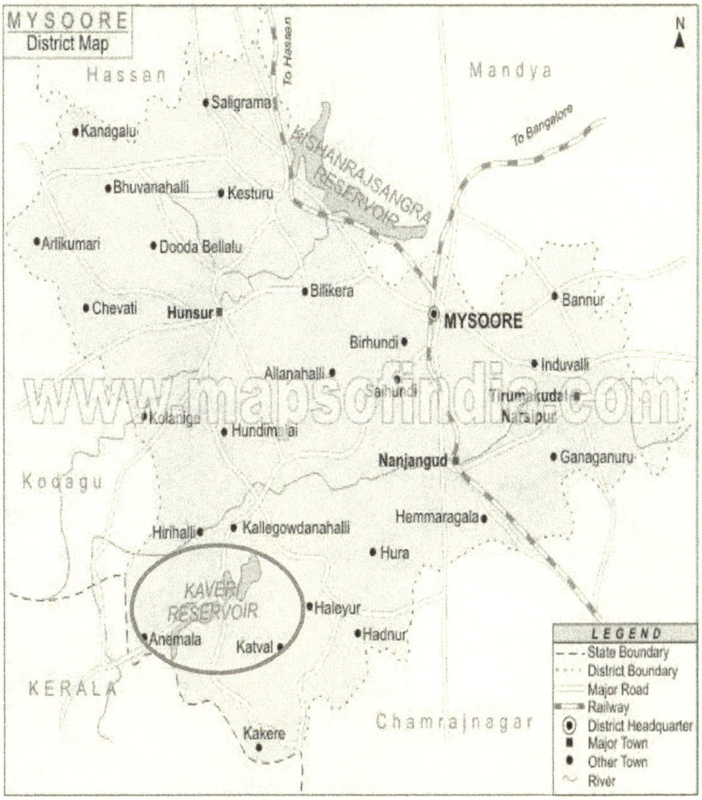

KODAGU

Kodagu is one of the smallest districts in Karnataka comprising 3 taluks - Madikeri, Somwarpet and Virajpet. Madikeri, a hill station, is the headquarters of Kodagu. Kodagu's greatest length from the Hemavathi river in the north to the Brahmagiri range in the south is about 96 kms and its greatest breadth from Sampaje in the west to Kushalnagar in the east is about 60 kms. The district has an area of 4,102 sq.km and 30 percent of the district is forest area.

Map- 4.2 : Map of Kodagu

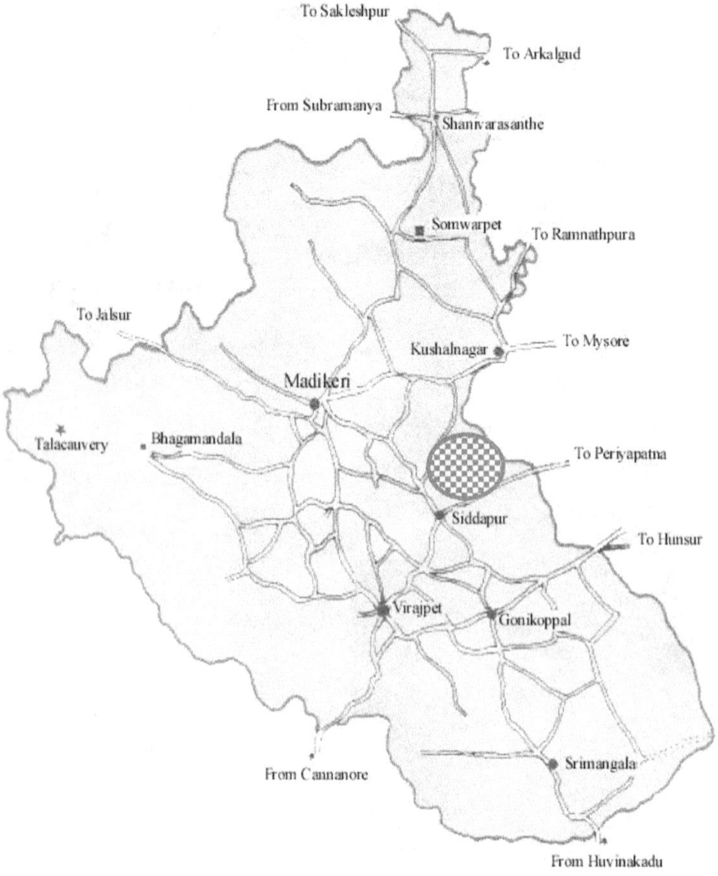

According to 1991 census, the total tribal population in the district is 40,300, which amounts to 8.25% of the total population of the district. There are 154 tribal colonies in which 4693 tribal families are residing. Jenukuruba, Bettakuruba, Kadukuruba, Kuruba, Yerava, Marata, Meda, Kudiya and Nayaka communities come under the perview of tribes in Kodagu district.

As per the census of 2001, the total population of the district is 5,51,000. In this population, 46,115 are tribal population in Kodagu. There are 28 Primary Health Centres, 2 Community Health Centres, 2 General Hospitals, 5 Primary Health Units and 2 Mobile Tribal Health Units under the control of District Health Officer. Besides this, there is one more District Hospital in Madikeri and two Taluk Hospitals situated in Somwarpet and Virajpet taluk under the direct control of Medical Directorate. Besides these communities, tribes such as Yeravas, Kurubas, Airies and Kudiyas, who are believed to be the original settlers of the area, also live in Kodagu (website of Kodagu District)

Table – 4.4 : Tribal Population Of Kodagu District

Particulars	Kodagu District Taluks			Total
	Madikeri	Somvarpet	Virajpet	
Population	5500	7300	27500	40300
Hadis	14	53	87	154
Families	668	979	3046	4693
Important sub-caste names of tribes	Kudiya, Maratha, Soliga, Nayaka	Yerava, Maratha, Meda, Soliga, Nayaka, Jenukuruba, Bettakuruba	Yerava, Maratha,Kuruba, Jenukuruba, Bettakuruba, Kadukuruba	

UTTAR KANNADA

Uttar Kannada is one of the industrially underdeveloped districts in Karnataka. The Halakki, as they are known in Uttar Kannada are the original inhabitants of the district. Scholars opine that the word Halakki is derived from the word Pallakki in Kannada (meaning - Palanquin). Halakki have distinct characteristics in their social customs, attire and their knowledge about herbal medicine (. Acharya, A.S 1967).

Prof. G.L. Bhat along with other scholars like Dr. Gowrish Kaikini and Dr. L.R. Hegde have done extensive research on the Halakki Tribe. Earliest documents about the tribe can be seen in 'Gazetteer of the Bombay Presidency – Vol. No. XV, Part I, Published in 1883. Dr. L.R. Hegde (1981) dealt extensively on home remedies practiced by Halakki tribes in his book (Kannada) "JANAPADA VAIDYA".

"Even today people come from far and wide to receive medical treatment for chronic disease conditions like herpes, liver problems to Halakki home remedies practitioners (Dr. G.L. Hegde, 1988).

Table – 4.5 : Halakki Hadi in Uttar Kannada

Halakki Hadi	Taluks in Uttar Kannada
36	Karvar
23	Ankola
76	Kumta (Hegde)
18	Honnavar

Table – 4.6 : Medical facilities in Uttar Kannada

.District	Total Population	Tribals Population	Doctor's Post sanctioned	Doctors working	Total Hospitals (PHC, CHC, Gen. Hospital)
Uttar Kannada	1,353,644	23,781	185	144	70

Source : Census of India 2001

Map - 4.3 : Map of Uttar Kannada

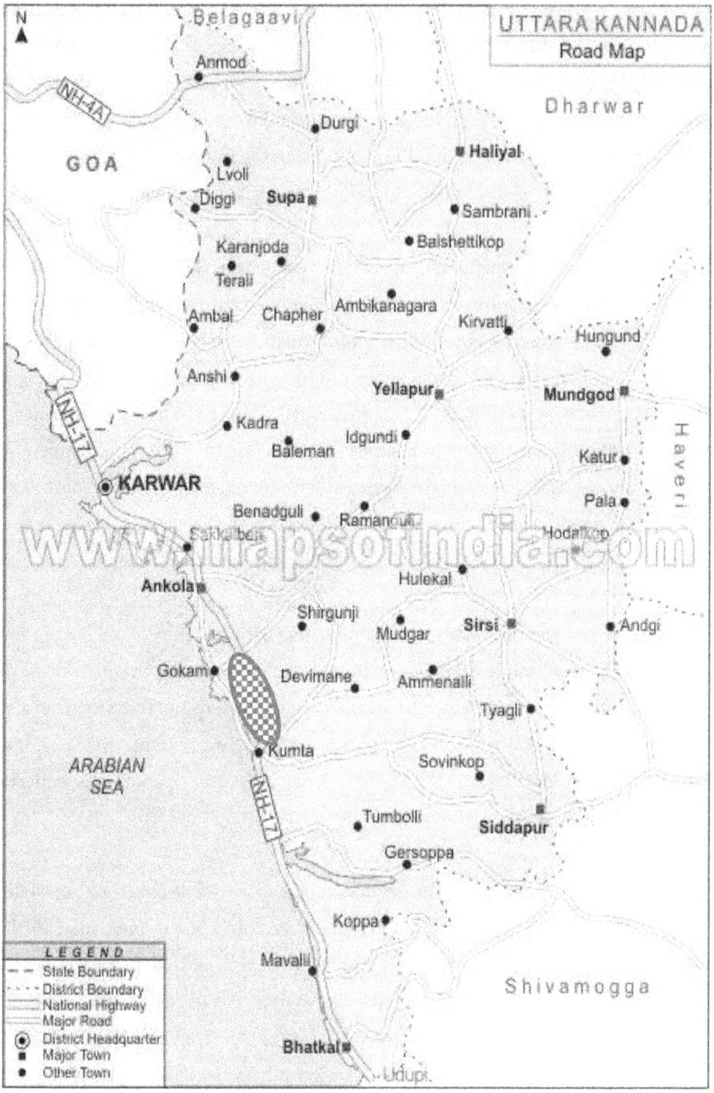

ANALYSIS AND INTERPRETATION

In any analysis it is essential to give a picture of the samples studied. Thus this section of the chapter provides with the sketches of the over all profile of the samples. In a proposition to ascertain the existent position with reference to the health care delivery system, a structured questionnaire was designed. Enlisted objectives of the study were kept in mind to elicit responses from various respondents. The data was coded and analyzed with the help of statistical technique.

This chapter contains a brief analysis of the tables relating to each question in the questionnaire. Tables are designed to facilitate an evocative interpretation. The questionnaire was administered separately to 535 samples. Samples consist of a good demographic mix. Samples were further segregated into school going tribal children, tribal adults and health care professionals serving in health care centers in tribal belts. Subjects were asked to complete the questionnaire except in the case of tribal school going children. Tribal schoolteachers completed on behalf of tribal school going children. This chapter constitutes the body of the study to arrive at a conclusion. A great deal of care has been exercised to observe utmost accuracy.

Health condition of school going tribal children is considered as a parameter in the study as deterioration of health would force the tribal child to discontinue the schooling. Schoolteachers in tribal schools were interviewed to examine the health status of 200 tribal school going children. Total sample was 200, out of which 97 were tribal boys and 103 were tribal girls. Information was collected from tribal primary schools.

Tribal adults interview focused on the impact on disability burden on individual, household and economic activity compromised due to ill health. Total sample of tribal adults was 300 out of which 147 were male and 153 female tribal adults. It was also to examine the impact of existing system and their options with dealing with them. How tribal envisaged the intervention of primary health care in emergency and their views on preventive services and health promotion did form the theme. Their views on improving the existing system were found out. Questionnaire was also designed to record their traumatic experience dealing with health care professional. Sought the views for an inclusive, empathetic institutional environment in Health care center.

Health care professionals were interviewed to seek their opinion to examine the participatory approach and environmental hurdles in implementing the programmes. Total no of sample was 35. There was an inherent limitation with regard to samples of Health care professionals as the number of health care centers in and around tribal areas is very small. Subjects were requested to complete the questionnaire consisting of various themes.

Consistent with the wise axiom "Prevention is better than cure" the questions underpinned the theme of prevention of diseases and modalities. Other sections included were broader approaches on flexible yet practical issues, inherent passion to work in rural areas, difficulty faced by the workers, role of technical assistance, training, infrastructure development, to mention a few.

Profile of sample –Tribal school children

Researcher in a Tribal School

Table – 5.1: Attendance of tribal children at school

Attendance	Boys	Girls	Total
<20 %	2	1	3
	2.1%	1.0%	1.5%
21 -30 %	2	5	7
	2.1%	4.9%	3.5%
31-50 %	41	45	86
	42.3%	43.7%	43.0%
51-80 %	52	52	104
	53.6%	50.5%	52.0%
>81%	0	0	0
Total	97	103	200

Diagram -5.1

Attendance of Tribal children at school

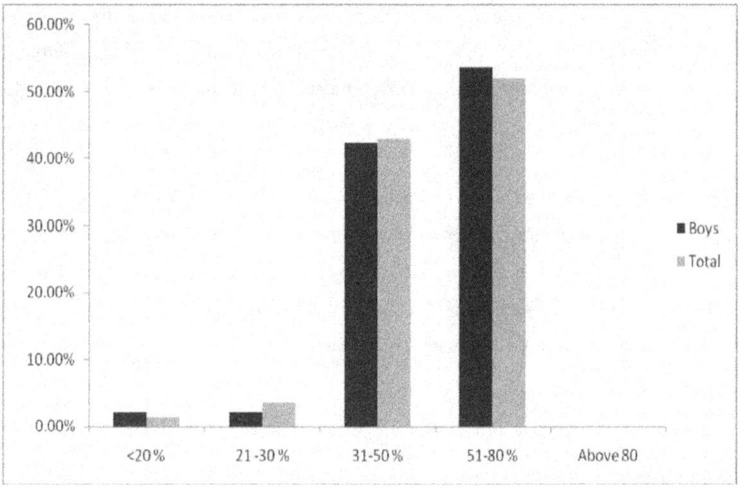

The above table is focused on the attendance of tribal children in school. It is obvious from the above table that no child had the full attendance in the school.

It was observed that only 52% of tribal school children had an attendance between 50-80 %(Table No 5.1). It goes without saying that during the formative age of school children where sound foundation of learning is needed, cent percent attendance in school is essential. It is crucial in the case of tribal school children because their parents are also illiterate. There has been an ever-increasing amount of research positively linking parent's education to encouragement to schooling the children. This is partly due to the conducive environment created by parents at home for children to study.

Teachers also gave their opinion that only 43 % of the school children had class attendance of 30-50 %. Multitudes of events make tribal school children to remain absent in the school. One of the major factors is sickness. Good health is an important factor for school going children.

It is important to notice that a small percentage of school going children (5%) had less than 30 percent of attendance. This is indicative of changing attitude of tribal parents recognizing the importance of schooling their children. It appears that incessant campaign by Government agencies on educating their children is paying dividends.

It can also be observed from the table 5.1 that there was no marked difference between the number of boys and girls in terms of attendance in the school. Basic education incontrovertibly forms the foundation for a stable and promising life. Hence, it is essential that reasons for tribal children to remain absent in school are identified and addressed sensitively.

Table – 5.2: Reasons for absence from the school

Reason for Absence	Boys	Girls	Total
Total No of Students	97	103	200
Other Reason	0	6	6
%	0	5.8%	3.0%
Harvesting	16	21	37
%	16.5	20.4%	18.5%
Distance	0	1	1
%	0	1.0%	5%
Discouragement	52	35	87
%	53.6	34%	43.5%
Sickness	29	40	69
%	29.9	38.8%	34.5%

The table 5.2 indicates that sickness (34.5 %) is the second most important reason for the tribal students to remain absent from school, next only to the discouragement factor (43.5%) from parents. "Teachers opined that minor injuries and stomach upset are the common reasons for the children to stay back at home". (Mandal Commission, 2006).

Besides, sickness makes school children less attentive in the school and makes them irritable. Compromised reflexes may dampen the grasping ability of school children in the school. Therefore, a long history beginning with poor schooling precedes illiteracy of tribals in the modern era.

Table – 5.3: Health status of tribal school children

Chronic Illness	Boys	Girls	Total
Yes	27	40	67
%	27.8%	38.8%	33.5%
No	70	63	133
%	72.2%	61.2%	66.5%
Total	97	103	200
%	100%	100%	100%

Diagram -5.2

Health status of tribal school children

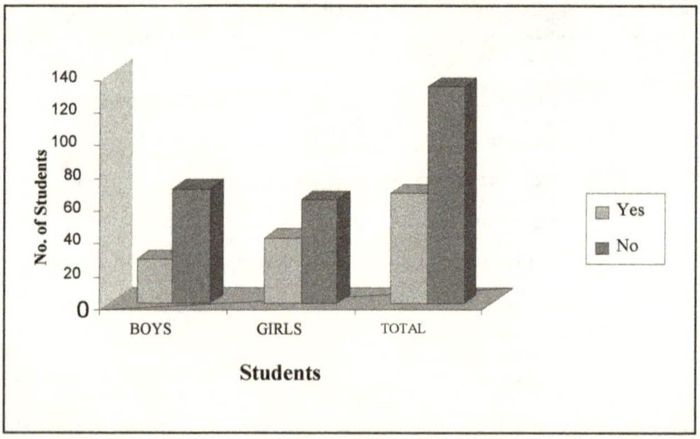

During the survey, teachers of the tribal schools reported that 66.5% of the school children have maintained overall good health. Teachers also opined that the students who maintain good health display high levels of mental alertness. These healthy students display enthusiasm in the course of learning. Good physical activity on playground is one more characteristic shown by these healthy students.

It is important to note that often these healthy students have shown very desirable changes in studies compared to their unhealthy counterparts. These behavioral indicators are not uncommon in growing age.

So far as number of students with poor health is concerned, 33.5% of the children suffered from poor health (Table 5.3). Of the total of 200 school children when a sex-wise analysis was made the scenario was delineated as mentioned below. Among them 38.8 % of the school children were girls, who had chronic debilitating conditions like anemia, dry cough and fungal infections. Only 27.8% of the boys had such chronic ill health (Table No 5.3).

A deeper analysis of consequences of poor health among students throw light on the fact that the healthy students could tend to air feelings of dominance due to over all pleasant response they receive compared to their counterparts who have poor health condition. Often students with poor health tend to be over submissive.

It is important to note that the health of school going children has a relevance in the community. This emphasizes the fact that there is a need to sensitize the policy makers about the ground reality of unhealthy conditions of school going tribal children

Table – 5.4: General unhealthy signs observed

	Boys		Girls		Total	
Healthy	26	26.8%	37	35.9%	63	31.5%
Pot belly	53	54.6%	40	38.8%	93	46.5%
Cough	4	4.1%	5	4.9%	9	4.5%
Fungal Infection	7	7.2%	15	14.6%	22	11.0%
General Weakness	7	7.2%	6	5.8%	13	6.5%
Total	97	100%	103	100%	200	100%

During the survey with the Tribal schoolteachers with regard to signs and symptoms of chronic sickness, teachers assessed that 46.5 % of the school children had potbelly, which could be mostly attributed to untreated worm infections. Physiological symptoms of potbelly were apparent (Table No 5.4).

Medical literature reveals that Hookworm infection which is a predominant cause of anemia (a condition of reduced Hemoglobin count in blood) and protein depletion is due to barefoot walk. Round worms infection was very common which is waterborne. Most of the tribal school children suffer from roundworm infection. Untreated worm infection may lead to vague stomachache, fatigue, disturbance in sleep and most importantly loss of enthusiasm. A diet of low protein and worm infection will hamper physical growth. Children with reduced immune and body defense can be susceptible to infections often. And it is this unhealthy condition that will make school going tribal children remain absent from school.

It is not surprising that while potbelly was observed more in boys, fungal infection was more in girls. It was probably due to boys going around and eating outside more frequently than girls.

Fungal infection was observed in 11 % of the children (Table No 5.4). Poor physical hygiene could be a predisposing factor for fungal infection. Teachers also informed that recurrent fungal infections are not uncommon due to poor body resistance due to general weakness.

It was revealed in the survey that 68.5% of school children had one or the other symptoms of unhealthy condition on as against 31.5% healthy school children (Table No 5.4). A good health is a fundamental human need. Tribal schoolteachers also brought out the fact that most of the disease conditions in school children from suffering from are preventable and have their roots in malnutrition and unhygienic living conditions.

Diagram -5.3

General unhealthy signs observed

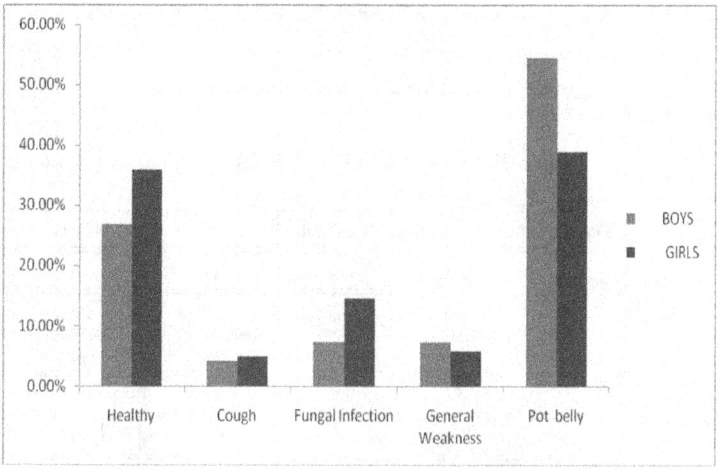

Table –5.5: Frequency of sickness

Frequency	Boys	Girls	Total
Occasionally	86	83	169
%	88.7%	80.6%	84.5%
Twice	10	16	26
%	10.3	15.5%	13%
Thrice	1	4	5
%	1.0%	3.9%	2.5%
Total	97	103	200
%	100%	100%	100%

As assessed by teacher of the Tribal school 13 % of the school children fell ill twice in last one year and required medical advice. Among the school children only 2.5% of the children experienced sickness thrice in current year due to which they remained absent in school (Table No 5.5).

It would be apt to mention here that condition of good health is more than mere absence of disease .It is a state of total psychological and social well being too of an individual in a given social environment. While psychologically frequent sickness can hamper the confidence level of a student and it can physically incapacitate to adapt to new learning environment.

Table – 5.6 : No. of tribal children who received treatment and medicine

Treatment and Medicine Received	Boys	Girls	Total
Yes	56	68	124
%	57.7 %	66%	62%
No	41	35	76
%	42.3%	34%	38%
Total	97	103	200
%	100%	100%	100%

During the survey, teachers of the school reported that 62 % of the Tribal school children sought medical advice and took treatment (Table No 5.6). It is a welcome development that these school children were taken to health care center and medical treatment was sought. Many a time, it is the tribal schoolteacher who notices the severity of the symptoms of disease conditions and alerts the respective tribal parents. It is also a fact that tribal parents are busy and overlook the symptoms and take a note of it when the condition turns severe.

Among sick school children 38 percent did not go to seek treatment, instead took home remedies. It can be observed that even today tribals wish to take medical treatment with their home remedies. In the event that symptoms do not come under control, then they rush to health clinics for treatment. Among those who did not go to health clinics 34 % were girls(Table No 5.6)..

Table – 5.7 Complete medical investigations

Investigations	Boys		Girls		Total	
Yes	19	19.6%	22	21.4%	41	20.5%
No	78	80.4%	81	78.6%	159	79.5%
Total	97	100%	103	100%	200	100%

As assessed by the Teachers of Tribal School only 20.5 % of the School children had their thorough medical investigations done and 79.5 % of the School children did not undergo any medical investigations and just had received symptomatic treatment(Table No 5.7).

Various factors would play a role in parents not taking their children for medical examination. Teachers also opined that all those who underwent complete medical investigation had very severe symptoms of disease condition. They may vary from simple negligence to undeniable poor socioeconomic conditions. The important factor to be noted here that tribal parents may not be aware of the importance of investigation and end up in a clinic of an unqualified medical practitioner giving symptomatic relief to their children.

Apart from distance to health care centers from tribal settlement, poverty remains the single most important discouraging factor to rush their children to health care centers.

Table – 5.8 : Maintenance of medical records

Maintenance	Treatment and Medicine Records		Total
	Boys	Girls	
Yes	2	4	6
%	2.1%	3.9%	3%
No	95	99	194
%	97.9%	96.1%	97%
Total	97	103	200
%	100%	100%	100%

As observed by the school teachers only 3 % of the Tribal school children had maintained records for the treatment received from medical professionals when they fell ill and 97 % of the school children that visited hospital had no records with them at all(Table No 5.8).

It is obvious from the table that tribals have inadequate knowledge about the importance of preserving medical records. It is a fact that the previous medical records help a medical practitioner to come into grip with the present ailment quicker than without the medical records. Previous records would save time in case of emergency.

Profile of sample-tribal adults

Researcher conducting the interview with tribals

Table – 5.9 Immediate health care consultation

	Sex		Total
	Male	Female	
Only Tribal doctor	39	34	73
	26.5%	22.2%	24.3%
Both Tribal doctor and Govt Hosp.	84	76	160
	57.1%	49.7%	53.3%
Only Govt Hosp	24	43	67
	16.3%	28.1%	22.3%
Total	147	153	300
	100%	100%	100%

This table gives a clear picture that 24.3 % of the respondents chose to visit only the tribal doctors to seek medical advice at the time of their sickness. But, almost an equal number of respondents 22.3 % said that they would like to go to Government hospital only and 53.3 % of the respondents were indecisive and said that they would seek medical advice from both Tribal and Government health professionals (Table No 5.9).

It is obvious from the table that tribal medicine is still predominantly practised in tribal society. Almost half of the respondents are not averse to visit tribal doctors for the medical treatment. But respondents from younger age group of tribal were decisive and wished to go to government hospital only. This suggests that awareness about the benefits of modern health care system is growing among the younger generation of tribals.

Table – 5.10 : Health cause to visit the hospital

Nature of Health problem	Sex		Total
	Male	Female	
Common Ailment	0	1	1
	0	0.7	0.3
Work related problem	59	50	109
	40.1%	32.7%	36.3%
children	29	70	99
	19.7%	45.8%	33%
Emergency accident	11	4	15
	7.5%	2.6%	5%
Old Age Problems	48	28	76
	32.7%	18.3%	25.3%
Total	147	153	300
	100%	100%	100%

Diagram -5.4 Health cause to visit hospital

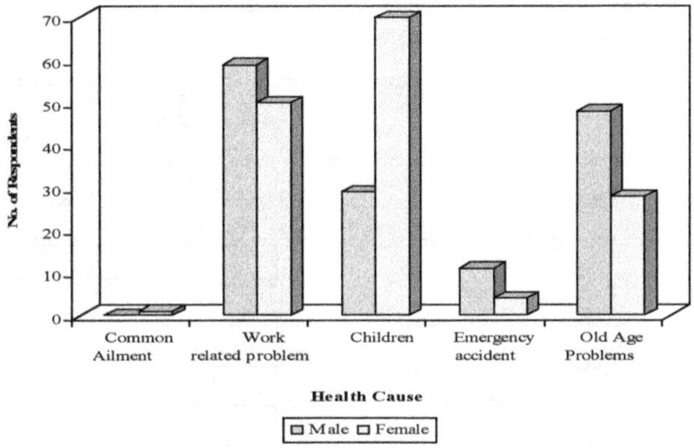

The above table shows that 36.3 % of respondents said that work related problems made them seek the advice of medical professionals (Table No 5.10). Since the primary occupation of the tribals is agriculture besides collecting forest produce, minor injuries during the monsoon season are common. Occasional falls from the tree have also been noticed.

It was not surprising that 33 percent said that it was sickness of children, which made them go for medical advice.

Almost a quarter of the respondents (25.3 percent) said that old age related health problems needed medical attention (Table No 5.10). As the tribals put in hard physical work during their lifetime, it was observed that most of the tribals suffer from one or the other physical ailment. Most of them were suffering from chronic arthritis (Pain in Joints) and symptoms of gastric ulcers (pain in the stomach) were very common. Respondents said that they wished to go to health care professionals to get these ailments treated.
As these conditions are chronic by nature they have to visit the health care centres regularly.

Table – 5.11: Home medicine in comparison to modern medicine

Comparison of Home Remedies	Sex		Total
	Male	Female	
Highly effective	27	23	50
	18.4%	15%	16.7%
Effective	48	38	86
	32.7%	24.8%	28.7%
Similar	46	65	111
	31.3%	42.5%	37%
Ineffective	26	27	53
	17.7%	17.6%	17.7%
Very ineffective	0	0	0
	0	0	0
Total	147	153	300
	100%	100%	100%

The above table reveals the perception of the tribals about the treatment with tribal medicines with that with modern medicines. Among the respondents 16.7 % of the respondents said that home remedies, which were traditionally used, were highly effective. In all 45.4 percent of the tribal respondents opined that their traditional treatment was effective even today (Table No 5.11). It is also a fact that unless the symptoms of the diseases conditions are very severe and unbearable, the tribals wish to use their own home medicine. It is the age-old practice and experience that many of their common ailments tribals have their own medicine.

Then, 37 percent of the respondents said both modern and traditional medicines were equally effective and it was not possible to prefer one to the other between the two systems of medicine. But 17.7% among the tribal respondents from the younger age group said that the home remedies were ineffective and modern medicines were much better.

Diagram –5.5 Home medicine and comparison

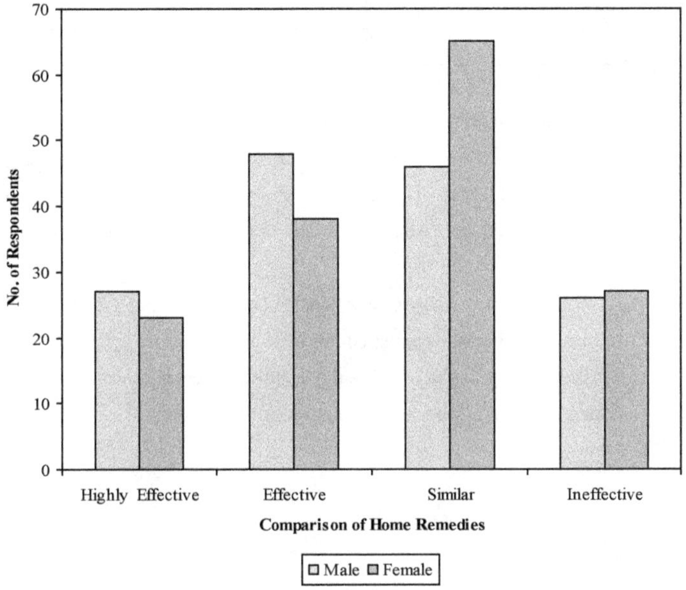

Table – 5.12 : Frequency of visits to government hospital for treatment

	Sex		Total
	Male	Female	
Not visited	24	4	28
	16.3%	2.6%	9.3%
Once	47	58	105
	32%	37.9%	35%
Twice	39	67	106
	26.5%	43.8%	35.3%
Many Times	12	10	22
	8.2%	6.5%	7.3%
Do Not Remember	25	14	39
	17%	9.2%	13%
Total	147	153	300
	100%	100%	100%

Among the Tribal respondents, 35.3 % and 35% had visited the hospital twice and once respectively. Only 9.3 % of the respondents had not visited even once. It can also be noted that only a small number of patients (2.6%) among the female respondents had not visited health care centers in the last one year (Table No 5.12).

It is interesting to note that among the visiting group of respondent female group visited more compared to their male counterpart. This suggests that lady patients had to visit more often the health care center either for themselves or for their young children to seek medical advice.

Table – 5.13 : Reasons to visit government hospital

Reasons	Sex		Total
	Male	**Female**	
Absence of Tribal doctor	31	11	42
	21.1%	7.2%	14.0%
Difficulties to manage with home remedies	57	82	139
	38.8%	53.6%	46.3%
Emergency	15	31	46
	10.2%	20.3%	15.3%
Life Threatening situations	17	29	45
	11.6%	19.0%	15.0%
Other reasons	27	0	27
	18.4%	0	9.0%
Total	147	153	300
	100%	100%	100%

It can be seen from the table (Table No 5.13) that a significant number of tribals first use the home (Native) medicine. Among the respondents 46.3% said that they wished to go to a Government hospital only when their home remedies fail to respond and another 14 % of the respondents said that they wished to visit Government hospital when tribal doctor was absent in the haadi. The above table also confirms that 30.3 percent of tribals go to Government hospital only when health conditions are life threatening and very serious, owing to emergencies. Emergencies generally arise from unforeseen occurrences. Eg. Accidents, insect bite etc.

Table – 5.14 : Recent experience with government hospital visit

	Sex		Total
	Male	Female	
Reached and treatment received	47	48	95
	32.0%	31.4%	31.7%
Did not reach in time	38	35	73
	25.9%	22.9%	24.3%
Medical Staff absent	8	7	15
	5.4%	4.6%	5.0%
Medicine not available	12	16	28
	8.2%	10.5%	9.3%
Doctor not available	42	47	89
	28.6%	30.7%	29.7%
Total	147	153	300
	100%	100%	100%

Diagram -5.6 : Recent experience with government hospital visit

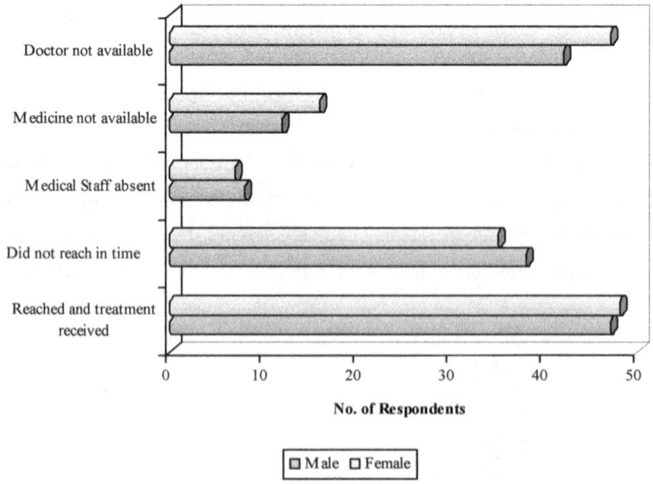

This question was addressed to the respondents to elicit their overall experience when they visited a health care centre to seek medical assistance. Among the respondents, 31.7% had reached the health care centre in time and received treatment but 24.3 % of the respondents could not reach in time (Table No 5.14). It was revealed that the distance by road from the tribal settlement was the main reason for their not being able to reach the centre in time. Transportation systems are not convenient to reach health care centers. Most of the respondents did not have a clear picture about the working hours in the health care centers. Many of the respondents expressed that working hours in health care centers as "two hours before and after lunch. Poor practice of punctuality owing to illiteracy is also an contributing factor for tribal patients to reach late.

It can also be seen from the Table that 29.7 % of the respondents could not receive medical treatment as doctors were not available to treat them and 9.3 % of the respondents experienced non availability of the medicine (Table No 5.14). In most of the cases, in such health care centers health care staff like doctors, nurses, pharmacists do not stay in the hospital vicinity. Health care staff commutes from their residence located in taluka or district head quarters. During monsoon seasons commutation to the health care centers located in remote areas becomes all the more difficult.

Even, today there are not frequent buses to these remote places. Although there has been increased governmental attention and media support for tribal health care centers in tribal area over the years but plan implementation and delivery appears to have overlooked the ground realities and the need of the tribal patients.

Table – 5.15 : Response from health service staff

Response	Sex		Total
	Male	Female	
Excellent	1	0	1
	7%	0	0.3%
Good	8	15	23
	5.4%	9.8%	7.7%
Fair	26	29	55
	17.7%	18.9%	18.3%
Poor	68	57	125
	46.3%	37.3%	41.7%
Very poor	44	53	96
	29.9%	33.7%	32.0%
Total	147	153	300
	100%	100%	100%

Detection of grievances and solutions can motivate the tribals to seek modern health care. Table shows that 73.7 % of the respondents received poor response (poor and Very poor category) from health service staff in the hospital and 26.3 % of the respondents opined that there was a good response (Good and Fair) when they visited health care centers (Table No 5.15).

"Patients usually do not visit Primary Health Centers in the early stages of their diseases, while healthcare providers (if at all present) are forced to focus only on seriously ill patients due to the volume of cases." (Neesha Patel 2005)

Table – 5.16 : Facilities availed during sickness

Facilities availed	Sex		Total
	Male	Female	
Can't say	38	28	66
	25.9%	18.3%	22.0%
Treatment given	30	31	61
	20.4%	20.3%	20.3%
Did not medicate in time	39	42	81
	26.5%	27.5%	27.0%
Fees unmanageable	12	9	21
	8.2%	5.9%	7.0%
Doctor/ staff unavailable	19	25	44
	12.9%	16.3%%	14.7%
Could not afford to buy medicines prescribed	9	18	27
	6.1%	11.8%	9.0%
Total	147	153	300
	100%	100%	100%

Respondents' experience, when they visited health care centers, to seek medical advice is depicted in this table. This table reveals that 20.3 % of the respondents could avail of medical advice when they were ill. Another 27 % of the respondents had received treatment but it was late and they had to suffer due to delayed medication(Table No 5.16). As discussed earlier, sometimes procrastination to visit healthcare center makes the tribal pay a heavy price. Facility of transportation also is poor. Subsequent to uncontrolled infection following administration of tribal medicines, tribal patients would be compelled to approach modern health care centers. Consequently tribal patients reach rather late to seek treatment from qualified health care professionals. There were 9 % of the respondents who could not afford to buy the medicines from private medical stores owing to cost. Poor tribals would come to seek medical advice with the notion that treatment is free of cost. Due to poor inventory of medicine in health care centers tribal patients, sometimes, receive only prescriptions of drugs, which have to be brought from private firms. These unexpected circumstances may end up with either the patient not buying the prescribed quantity of medicine in full or may not buy at all. The risk envisaged in both cases is that visit to seek medical advice would be futile without a cure for the ailment.

Diagram – 5.7 : Facilities availed during sickness

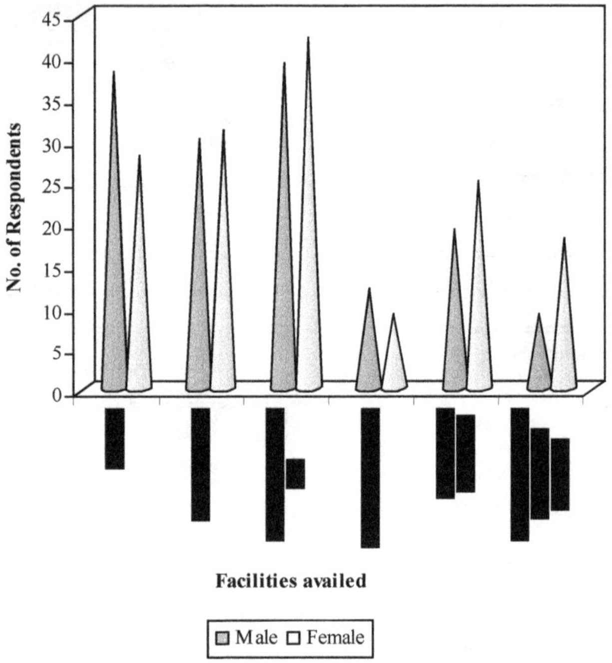

Table – 5.17: Problems faced in seeking medical treatment

	Sex		Total
	Male	Female	
Distance	54	63	117
	36.7%	41.2%	39%
Fees	21	31	52
	14.3%	20.3%	17.3%
Treatment ineffective	18	12	30
	12.2%	7.8%	10%
Unavailability of Doctor	27	43	70
	17.6%	29.3%	23.3%
Unavailability of Medicine	11	20	31
	7.5%	13.1%	10.3%
Total	147	153	300
	100%	100%	100%

Among the tribal respondents, 39 % felt that distance was the prohibitive factor in their efforts to seek timely medical advice. The next hindering factor (23.3%) was that health care professionals were not available when they visited the hospital. It is not surprising that female members of the survey samples expressed more than their male counterparts the unavailability of the health care professionals. Fees were also a discouraging factor as reported by 17.3 % of the respondents (Table No 5.17). It is expected that health care services in government health care centers are rendered free of cost. Many other studies also have reported similar incidences of collecting fees in government health care centers. Besides, demoralizing effect tribal patients may wait till such time as they gather enough money to visit health care centers. In many cases exacerbation of disease would have occurred. Sometimes late visit cost them dearly.

Table – 5.18: Death in the family during 1998 -2007

	Sex		Total
	Male	Female	
Don't Remember	38	28	66
	25.9%	18.3%	22.0%
> 71 years	42	52	94
	28.6%	34.0%	31.3%
51 to 70 years	51	50	101
	34.7%	32.7%	33.7%
21-50 Years	13	9	22
	8.8%	5.9%	7.3%
< 20 years	1	1	2
	0.7%	0.7%	0.7%
Infant and Child	2	13	15
	1.4%	8.5%	5.0%
Total	147	153	300
	100%	100%	100%

From the above table 31.3 % of the respondents stated that recent death of the family member occurred when that member was above 70 years of age. According to 33.7 % of the respondents, members in their families were between the age of 50 to 70 years when they died. But 5 of the respondents said there were deaths of infants and children in their families and 7.3 % of the respondents stated there were deaths of youngsters between 20-50 years of age. Among the respondents 5 % of the respondents said that there were deaths of infants in their families as the infants could not get the immediate medical advice and treat the infants (Table No 5.18).

"The health status of the tribal population is not on par with the rest of the state's population. The infant mortality rate (IMR) of STs (64.37) is much higher than the state average (52.0)" (Status of Scheduled Tribes in Karnataka).

Table – 5.19 Timely treatment could have avoided the death

	Sex		Total
	Male	Female	
Don't know	38	28	66
	25.9%	18.3%	22.0%
Strongly Agree	15	24	39
	10.2%	15.7%	13.0%
Agree	67	79	146
	45.6%	51.6%	48.7%
Neither agree nor disagree	27	22	49
	18.4%	14.4%	16.3%
Disagree	0	0	0
	0	0	0
Strongly Disagree	0	0	0
	0	0	0
Total	147	153	300
	100%	100%	100%

From the earlier table it is evident that for various reasons it is difficult to reach the hospital in time and seek medical treatment. Therefore, this particular question in the above table was addressed to respondents to assess their perception about a possible avoidance of a recent death if timely medical assistance had been provided.

Among the respondents, 61.7 percent gave their opinion that death could have been avoided. While 16.3 percent of respondents preferred to remain neutral as they were not able to decide the impact of unavailability of immediate and timely access to health care(Table No 5.18).

Table – 5.20 : Proper medical care could have averted infant mortality

	Sex		Total
	Male	**Female**	
Don't know	127	97	224
	86.4%	63.4%	74.7%
Definitely True	0	22	22
	0	14.4%	7.3%
Probably True	12	26	38
	8.2%	17.0%	12.7%
Not Sure	7	7	14
	4.8%	4.6%	4.7%
Probably Not	0	1	1
	0	0.7%	0.3%
Definitely Not	1	0	1
	0.7%	0	0.3%
Total	147	153	300
	100%	100%	100%

Difficulty to access the health care centre in an emeregency can lead to disastrous results especially in the case of infants and children . This is also due to the fact that this group (Infant and children) is the most susceptible group for casuality if immediate medical investigations and treatment are not given. That the children cannot speak and express their greivances and that parents have to narrate their observation is also an important dimension of the problem.

In this backdrop, question was posed to the respondents. It was revealed that 20 percent of the respondents expressed their opinion that death could have been avoided if children had been provided medication in time (Table No. 5.20).

Table – 5.21 : A good scheme to fulfill health care need

Good Scheme	Sex		Total
	Male	Female	
Only tribal doctor	0	0	0
	0	0	0
Both Tribal doctor and Govt Hosp	19	15	34
	12.9%	9.8%	11.3%
Govt Hosp with free medicine	52	56	108
	35.4%	36.6%	36.0%
Constant availability of a doctor in the area with free medicine	76	82	158
	51.7%	53.6%	52.7%
Total	147	153	300
	100%	100%	100%

Old age by itself is a limiting factor to access the health care center in time of need and seeking medical advice. From the above table it becomes evident that 52.7% of the respondents opined, it was necessary to have resident health care professionals with free distribution facility of the medicine (Table No 5.21).

Respondents were also conscious of the fact that medicinal equipments and drugs from private drug stores were unaffordable for them. Another 36% of the respondents gave the response that; there should be a government hospital in the proximity with facilities with free supply of medicine. Tribals also suggested that they should not be denied health care facilities for want of ability to pay. A general inference can be drawn from the table that there is a dearth of health care professionals, facilities and free medicine. A small number of 11.3 % of the respondents said they wished to have the services of both tribal and professional doctors (Table No 5.21).

PROFILE OF SAMPLE -HEALTH CARE PROFESSIONALS

Table –5.22 : Number of years of experience of health professionals

Yrs of Exp	2	3	4	5	6	7	8	9	10	12	14	15	22	28	30	Total
No	2	6	2	1	5	2	5	3	1	2	1	2	1	1	1	35
%	5.7	17.1	5.7	2.9	14.3	5.7	14.3	8.6	2.9	5.7	2.9	5.7	2.9	2.9	2.9	100

Table – 5.23 : Experience divided in years

Service Years	1-5 Years	6-10 Years	>11 Years	Total
No	10	17	8	35
Percentage	28.6	48.6	22.9	100

The experience of Health care professionals among respondents varied from 2 years to 30 years. There were 48.6 respondents with experience between 6-10 Years. And 22.9 percent of respondents had more than 10 years of experience of serving in tribal belts of Karnataka.

Table – 5.24 : Approach to hospitals from tribal settlements

Distance	By walk	Only by vehicle	Both	Total
Health Care Facility	2	19	14	35
Percentage	5.7	54.3	40	100

This question was put to health care professionals with the view that distance from residence of tribal settlements to health care clinics assumes a great importance for tribal patients in availing themselves of health care benefits in case of a health breakdown in general and an emergency in particular. Denial of easy access can be an independent factor for the reluctance of the tribal patients to seek medical advice and the consequent aggravation of the disease condition.

Table 5.24 indicates that there is a significant difference in number among the health care centers, which can be approached on foot and with the help of motor vehicles. Of the available health care centers, 54.3 percent of the health care centers were approachable only when a patient used transport system like bicycles, bullock cart or motor vehicles and only 5 .7 % of them could be reached on foot.

It can also be noted that 40 % of Health care centers could also be accessible both by walking on unconventional roads (like crossing hills or rivers) and circuitous motorable roads (Table 5.24).

Table – 5.25: Number of settlements dependent on health care professionals

No of Settlements	1-5	6-10	>10	Total
No of Health Care professionals	12	10	13	35
Percentage	34.3	28.6	37.1	100

Unequal distribution of health care professionals is the key factor, which hampers the effectiveness and responsiveness of health care delivery systems. It can be observed from Table 5.25 that 37.1 % respondents have dependency of more than 10 settlements each and 28.6 % respondents said 5 to 10 settlements depend on them for health care services. At times, beurocratic work like office administration, court duty to attend to medico –legal cases (To present the facts before judicial magistrate) cause delay in attending to the patients.

Organizational reporting system demands monthly meeting with their superiors, in taluka head quarters and sometimes with district medical officer (DMO) in district head quarters. This is, again, a causative factor for the unavailability of a medical officer in health care centers.

Public holidays, periodic training programmes in district headquarters, could be yet another reason and most importantly, difficulty to reach the health care centers due to transportation problems affects the services. Inadequate number of medical officers on one hand and unavailibity of them due to various reasons on the other hand would push the tribal patients to the state of despondency. Repeated experience of unavailability of medical officer in health care centers would force the tribal patients to land in the clinics of unqualified medical practitioners.

Table – 5.26 : Percentage of tribals treated among patients

No of Health Professionals	Tribals among patients	Percentage
6	30-50 %	17.1%
16	51-70%	45.7%
12	>71 %	34.3%
1	100 %	2.9%
35	Total	100%

In order to gain a greater insight into the health care delivery systems and productivity in terms of medical treatment received by tribal patients, health care professionals were surveyed from in and around the Tribal area.

Among the respondents 17.1% health care professionals opined that 30-50 percent of the patients that they treated were tribals and 45.7 percent of the respondents said that more than half the number of patients they treated everyday were tribals.34.3 percent of the health care professionals had above 70% of the tribals as their patients among the total no of the patients they treat everyday (Table 5.26).

This table depicts that tribal patients have very few health care centers to depend on .It is evident from the fact that many health care professionals expressed that their patients load consisted of significant number of tribal patients. Yet another fact is that these health care centers are surrounded by a number of non-tribal villages. Consequent overcrowding of patients in out patient department (OPD) would restrict the time to be utilized by health care professionals for diagnosis of disease. Tribal patients may not be left with enough time to exhibit the signs and describe the symptoms of the disease conditions he/she is suffering from.

Table – 5.27 : Facilities available to treat tribal patients

No of Health Care Professionals	Facilities	Percentage
0	Excellent	0
0	Very Good	0
4	Good	11.43%
7	Fair	20%
24	Poor	68.57%
Total N=35		100

Diagram - – 5.8 : Facilities available to treat tribal patients

Early detection of disease is said to be the most important step to help patients in arresting the progress of disease. Failing or delaying to detect diseases early, due to lack of laboratory facilities and non- availability of specialist's services at the required time can spell disaster for patients. In view of the importance of early detection, this question was asked.

Table 5.27 suggests that 68 % of health care professionals observe that facilities are poor and need urgent up- gradation as against 31 percent of the respondent who said they could manage with the existing facility. This suggests that the mere presence of a medical officer and basic infrastructure does not mean that services can be delivered efficiently and effectively. Although there has been increased outlay on the infrastructure emphasis on effective translation into benefits for those who are targeted is missing.

It is very crucial to check the imbalance between the required and the available facility. Minimum infrastructure facility required includes adequate number of medical and paramedical staff, laboratory facilities and continuous supply of drugs. Some of the health care professionals opined that most of the time their professional skills could be utilized, as adequate facilities were not available.

It has also come to light that lack of infrastructure causes a great deal of inconvenience for highly skilled health care professionals and consequently pushes them to the brink of dissatisfaction. It may also happen that health care professionals may continue with their services only out of compulsion. This has led many social researchers to perceive that dedication is very low on the part of health care professionals working in these tribal areas. However, these factors have a great negative effect on the quality of health care service delivery. Quick attention and faster response by government agencies to this lacuna may be important determinants to improve the quality of health service delivery.

Table – 5.28 : Modern treatment as first choice

No of Health Professionals	Voluntary Visit by Tribals	Percentage
2	Definitely True	5.7
7	Probably True	20
9	Not Sure	25.7
14	Probably Not	40
3	Definitely Not	8.6
	Total	100

Table above suggests that, 74.3 % Respondents reported that Tribals turn up to them for treatment only when all other mode of treatments at their disposals are exhausted (Table 5.28).

Only 5.7% of the respondents opined that Tribals came to them for the medical advice as a first choice. Respondents expressed their concern that patients do not visit the health care centers early to facilitate the treatment to be effective, timely and economical. Effective utilization of the available services depends on tribal perception of quality of modern health care services and preference. There is a direct relationship between the early visit of patient and total cost of health care services. Respondents stressed the need on educational campaign to increase the awareness of benefits about modern medicine among tribals.

"Besides poor coverage, the tribal communities have their own systems of medicines, dispensed through the medium of shamans, herbalists and witchdoctors, which also acts as a barrier in healthcare programmes " (A.K. Kalla et al 2004).

Table – 5.29 : Should health professionals visit tribal areas?

Vital to visit tribal areas to treat	No of Health Professionals	Percentage
Definitely True	23	65.7
Probably True	11	31.4
Not Sure	1	2.9
Probably Not	0	0
Definitely Not	0	0

Table 5.29 shows that 65.7 % of the respondents opined that Health professionals must go to Tribal area to address the health care needs of Tribals. It is also the experience during their long service that conditions like difficult geographical terrain, poverty, illiteracy and also gender bias deprive them of the health care benefits both in the early stages of infections and sudden need. Therefore, 97.1 % of the respondents felt that it was important to visit Tribal areas. Respondents were of the opinion that overall healthcare outcome could be improved when doorsteps delivery of healthcare services were integrated into rural health care system and manpower resource allocation was the key factor to achieve this objective.

It is also important to notice that only a very small percentage of respondents (2.9 %) reported that it was not necessary to visit Tribal area to treat them (Table 5.29).

Table – 5.30 How open are the tribals to new suggestions?

How open to new suggestions	No. of Respondents	%
Extremely receptive	2	5.7
Very receptive	16	45.7
Somewhat receptive	13	37.1
Not very receptive	4	11.4
Not at all receptive	0	0
Total	35	100

Table No 5.30 suggests that tribals are receptive and open to suggestions by health care professionals. 45.7 % of respondents gave opinion that the tribals were very receptive and 5.7 % said the tribals were extremely receptive. Only 11.4% of the respondents reported that the tribals were not receptive to the suggestions.

This openness of tribal, as reported by respondents exhibited in the study favours a transcendental priority of the tribal society. These characteristics will make it possible to learn about the thrust area. This feature supports the implementation of strategic reach of health care services to the vulnerable group. This remarkable attitude of tribals, which the respondents felt can be used to seek detailed information for an in depth study to know the hardship faced by tribal society to avail the modern health care services. Respondents appreciated this behavioral dimension of openness to new suggestions especially of the younger age group.

Table – 5.31: Importance of formal education

Need for Formal Education	No Of Respondents	%
Definitely True	21	60
Probably True	12	34.3
Not Sure	2	5.7
Probably Not	0	0
Definitely Not	0	0

Diagram - – 5.9 : Importance of formal education

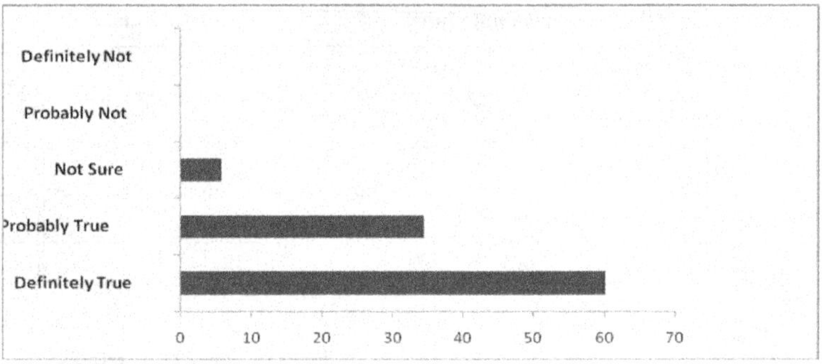

No. of Respondents

Education has a direct bearing on the progress of any society and it is aptly opined by 60% of the respondents that illiteracy was the root cause for tribals being deprived of the health care benefits (Table 5.31).

34.3 % of respondents suggested that it was probable that formal education could bring about changes (Table 5.31).

In all, 94.3 % of the respondents felt that education alone could make the tribal patients to appreciate the rational and scientific soundness of modern medicine and the importance of seeking early medical advice(Table 5.31).. Respondents opined that formal education would bring about changes in attitude, priorities and prefernces .Respondedents also expressed the fact that it was only the formal education which would make the tribal society concious of the advancements that were taking place in the medical world.

Survey also suggested that respondents were convinced of the fact that "formal education for all" must be implemented on a warfooting without which the expectation to reach the health careservices to this vulnerable group would remain a mirage.In a true sense formal education alone will sensitise the tribal society to the modern health care sytems and make them realise the instrumentality involved in healthcare services.

Table – 5.32: Passion to work for tribals

Passionate job	No. of Respondents	%
Strongly Agree	4	11.4
Agree	19	54.3
Neither agree nor disagree	6	17.1
Disagree	6	17.1
Strongly Disagree	0	0

Diagram –5.10: Passion to work for tribals

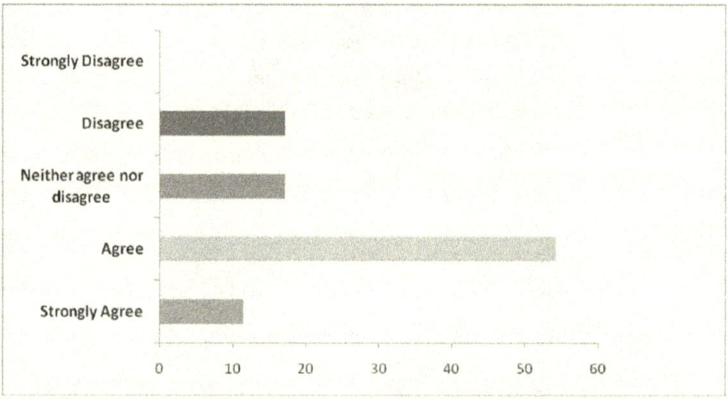

No. of Respondents

Expectations of the tribals from the health care services are increasing rapidly. Some of them are also aware of the service facilities made available in the health care centers in taluka health care centers and they expect a similar service with the health care center they visit. Lesser facilities available in health care centers can be compensated, to some extent when health care professionals exhibit an inherent passion to work for the tribals. Against this background this question on passion to work for tribals was asked. Professional excellence of health care professionals would be put into use only with the passion to serve in this area. An ambience of sympathetic, polite and human environment can be created in these deplorable centers of health care services only when functional responsibilities are discharged with passionate behavioral profile.

An overwhelming 54.3 % of the respondents during the survey agreed that they had a great liking for the job and to serve in a tribal area and 11.4 % of respondents said, they had a strong desire to work for the poor. But 17.1 % of the respondents gave a neutral opinion and other 17.1 % of them opined they were serving as a part of their service (Table 5.32).

In the current perspective, it was observed that 65 percent of respondents derived a great deal of professional satisfaction serving the tribals in rural area. However, a small percentage of respondents (17 .1 percent) said that they experienced difficulty in balancing their personal need and professional expectations (Table 5.32). This included employment of spouses, education of children, transportation facilities, poor social living etc.

"Among the factors conducive to the job performance, the feeling of worthwhile accomplishment was ranked the highest" (Laxmi Narain 1971).

Table – 5.33 : Free treatment facility

Free Treatment facility	**No. Of Respondents**	**%**
Strongly Agree	2	5.7
Agree	26	74.3
Neither agree nor disagree	6	17.1
Disagree	1	2.9
Strongly Disagree	0	0

Tribals are poor and cannot afford medical treatment when they are sick. The above table reveals that 80 percent of the respondents agree that tribal patients get their investigations, diagnosis, treatment and medicine free of cost in their health care center. But it was also revealed that 17.1 percent of the respondents remained silent. Among respondents 2.9 percent said that medical treatment was not free (Table 5.33).

In all, 20 percent of the respondents did not say categorically that treatment came to the patients free of cost. But the impact of "health services for cost" could cause a demoralizing effect on the tribal psyche. Paid health services can be an independent discouraging factor for tribals and can trap them in the vicious cycle of deprivation and despair.

A small fraction of the respondents (2.9 percent) vented their feeling that their counterparts with equal professional skills enjoyed a better standard of life in urban areas(Table 5.33). Hence, they collect a small amount as their professional fees for the service they rendered to patients.

Table – 5.34 : Accomplishment in treating sick tribals

No. of Respondents	Fulfillment	Percentage
2	Excellent	5.7
26	Very Good	74.3
6	Good	17.1
1	Fair	2.9
0	Poor	0
Total N=35		100

The Table 5.34 indicates that most of the respondents were affirmative. None gave a negative answer. In fact It can be noted that 5.7% of respondents said they were extremely happy as they were able to give a service to the best of their satisfaction to tribal patients who turned up to them seeking medical advice. A whooping 74.3 % of the respondents said health care service delivered to tribals from their end was very good and other 17.1 were satisfied that they were providing a good service to the patients.

A significant point to be noted is that health care centers are due for up-gradation for a long time. Decades of neglect by policy makers have virtually left the health care centers without sufficient resources. Of late, modern evolving technology considerably influences the services of hospitals. It is against this background that health care professionals in these centers are delivering reasonably decent services and are striving to accomplish the organizational goals.

Table – 5.35: Tribal patients are co- operative if you volunteer to give health care services

Tribals are cooperative	No. Of Respondents	%
Strongly Agree	0	0
Agree	1	2.9
Neither agree nor disagree	9	25.7
Disagree	21	60
Strongly Disagree	4	11.4
Total No	35	100

This question was posed to know the extent to which tribals are open to new ideas as compliance with drug regimen, suggested diet pattern, relevant exercises are of utmost importance. Sometime, health care professional's advice could appear unconventional to tribals and it is very important to understand the sensitivity involved in the interaction between a health care professional and tribals.

It is only 2.9 percent of the respondents agreed that tribals accept their professional advice whole-heartedly if they volunteer to treat. Astonishingly, 60 percent of the respondents said volunteering to serve evoke a poor response and 25.7 percent of the respondents did not give their opinion (Table 5.35). It can be emphasized here that the contours of patients –hospital relation have to undergo radical changes. Patients counseling has never been part of the treatment and integrated into health care services.

Table – 5.36 Overall health care service delivery to tribal patients

Overall health care service delivered	No. Of Respondents	%
Strongly Agree	4	11.4
Agree	26	74.3
Neither agree nor disagree	5	14.3
Disagree	0	0
Strongly Disagree	0	0
Total No	35	100

Diagram - 5.11 : Overall health care service delivery to tribal patients

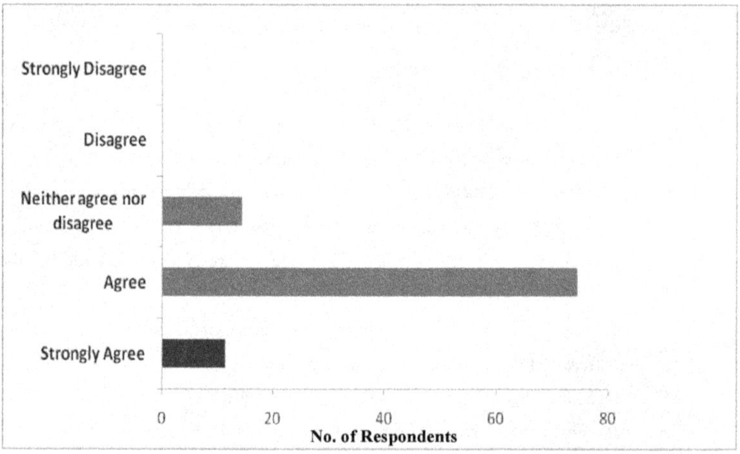

Although overall satisfaction of patients (over all productivity) is too complex a phenomenon to be measured with any single yard- stick, professional satisfaction experienced by Health care professionals can be an important component.

The table 5.36 indicates 74.3 % of the respondents agreed that they had been able to provide overall health care benefits to the tribal patients when the tribal patients approached health care centers and 11. 4% of the respondents opined that over all health care benefits to tribal patients was extremely good. But what is discouraging is that 14.3 % of the respondents were neutral.

Medical science is an ever-evolving field. Newer discovery of drugs, better diagnostic equipments do constantly help upgrade the service quality of professionls. Health care service has multidimensional distinctiveness. It is important to note that while private health care centers keep abreast of the latest medical equipments government hospitals receive the benefits of advanced technology very late due to the bureaucratic way of functioning.

In the absence of constant technological up gradation, the concept of consumer-satisfaction centered services in health care center alone would be a justification of accomplishing the task of health service delivery to the vulnerable poor. This table hypothesizes that overall health care delivery in the absence of modern facility lies in the time honored personalized services by identifying thrust areas like behavioral dimensions, detecting vulnerable segment of tribal, proactively approach epidemic infested areas etc

Table – 5.37: How well equipped to handle emergency?

Inadequately equipped to handle	No. Of Respondents	%
Cardiac Emergencies	1	2.9
Accidents	17	48.6
Contagious Diseases	10	28.6
Water born Epidemic break outs	7	20
Infants	0	0
Total	35	100

Nearly half of the respondents (48.6 %) are of the opinion that Tribal patients who are victims of accidents cannot be given adequate care, either due to late visits or the nature of the accidents. The diseases, which cannot be treated adequately, are contagious diseases and epidemic breakouts according to 28.6 % and 20 % of the respondents respectively (Table 5.37). Modernization efforts must primarily address the facilities on one hand and its delivery on the other. In the absence of modern medical investigative facility health care professionals are handicapped to deliver the services effectively. A constructive debate and discussion on this issue would address the constraints and limitation.

This observation of the respondents has a significant dimension. With inadequate infrastructure facilities the head of the organization or the senior most officer of the health care center has to motivate the employees constantly. This hypothesizes that seniors have to strive to mobilize the internal available resources in time of emergency. The seniors need to train and impress upon the juniors and the paramedical to enrich the behavioral profile with sympathy and empathy.

Table – 5.38 : Need for additional facilities

Need for Extra Facilities	No. of Respondents	%
Definitely True	18	51.4
Probably True	10	28.6
Not Sure	6	17.1
Probably Not	1	2.9
Definitely Not	0	0
Total	35	100

More than half of the respondents (51.4 %) said that it was definitely true that additional facilities were needed to provide a comprehensive health care to Tribal patients. Another 28.6 % said it was probably true that, with the additional facilities, patients could get much better health care benefits, which was lacking then. In all, 80 percent of respondents expressed their opinion that existing facilities were not adequate to treat the poor patients. Among the respondents, it was a small fraction of 2.9 percent, which felt that the existing facilities were enough and immediate up gradation was not needed. Inadequate facilities, respondents felt, creates a gap between services promised and services offered to the tribal patients.

"The Karnataka Lok Ayukta has estimated that at least 25 % of the budget is siphoned off through corrupt practices " (M H Rangegowda).

Table – 5.39 Effect of late visits to hospitals depriving the effective treatment

Delayed Visits impacts effective Treatment	No. of Respondents	%	Cumulative Percentage
A Great Deal	11	31.4	31.4
Quite A Lot	20	57.1	88.6
Some	3	8.6	97.1
Not Very Much	1	2.9	
Not At All	0	0	
Total	35	100	

The Early Bird concept occupies a place of pivotal importance in diagnosis and treatment of disease. The survey also suggests that 31.4% of the respondents feel that it is greatly, the late visits that deprive the tribals of the effective and timely treatment. Almost all respondents (97.1) said that in most cases, inadequate health care was due to late visits (Table 5.39).

Respondents expressed the opinion that failing to identify the reason would make the task of orchestrating available resources difficult. On one hand tribals need to be sensitized on the need of early visit (without lapsing time) and on the other there should be optimizing the resources available at their disposal to meet the emergency need. Responsibility of developing general awareness among the tribals must be shouldered by the government .The pace of sensitization can be activated with innovative devices of promotion like slogans, posters in important points, messages related to healthcare, regular counseling etc. Late visits of patients to health care centers can cause heavy damage, health care professionals have to exhibit creativity at its best.

Table – 5.40 : Patients buying medicines from private drug Stores

Patients Buy medicine from Private Drug stores	No. of Respondents	%
Definitely True	9	25.7
Probably True	11	31.4
Not Sure	15	42.9
Probably Not	1	2.9
Definitely Not	0	0
Total	35	100

Among the respondenets, 57.1% reported that the burden to purchase medcine, following diagnosis became the resonsibility of the patients(Table 5.40). Patients have to buy medicines from private medical shops either due to the nonavailabilty of a particular medicine or for an advanced molecule (Latest medicine).

Among the respondents 42.9 percent were indecisive and preferred to remain neutral (Table 5.40). Respondents agreed that while they were expected to work with an avowed mission of sincerety and personal commitment, it was the circumstances which made them use drugs from outside. Health care communication system ,respondents said that,in rural areas was not still active. Poor inventory is the root cause.The supplies of essential medicines need to be properly channelised. In times of epidimics and natural calamities it is an ignominy, if government administration does not ensure supplies on priority basis.

Respondents said that they were aware that patients turned up to them with great hopes ,some times after visiting unqualified doctors and it was their helplessness due to shortage of drugs that pateints were asked to buy medicines from outside.

Table – 5.41: Inadequacy in provision of vital health care

Health care benefits missing	No. of Respondents	%	Cumulative Percentage
A Great Deal	3	8.6	8.6
Quite A Lot	16	45.7	54.3
Some	12	34.3	88.6
Not Very Much	3	8.6	97.1
Not At All	1	2.9	
Total	35	100	

Cumulatively, no of respondents who opined from "some tribal patients to most tribal patients" stood at 88.6 % and 54.3 % respondents said, quite a lot of patients were missing vital health care benefits (Table 5.41). Respondents were of the opinion that a host of reasons deprive the tribal patients miss out of many benefits. In recent years, government has tried to conceptualize the emerging healthcare need of vulnerable poor and prioritized several initiatives. Some of them include increasing human resource, improved infrastructure, training and development, campaigns etc.

Further discussion with respondents revealed that the organizational instruments were yet to develop a strong sense of realization. This has caused a major fall in the productive efficacy of health care delivery system. In order to bring about a qualitative transformation it is imperative that functional areas like health care services, transportation, and campaign on formal education are aligned.

"Unfortunately, in India, not only is there pre-existing inequality in healthcare provisions, but this is further enhanced by difficulties in accessing it, which is due to geographical, socio-economic or gender distance"(Neesha Patel 2005).

Table – 5.42: Need of specialist doctor services

Need for Specialists	No. of Respondents	%
Strongly Agree	10	28.6
Agree	18	51.4
Neither agree nor disagree	6	17.1
Disagree	1	2.9
Strongly Disagree	0	0
Total No	35	100

Among the respondents 80% agreed that there was a need for specialist doctors for comprehensive health care in tribal area. Only 2.9 % of the respondents disagreed with the concept that specialist's services were needed. But a good number of respondents namely 17.1 percent remained indecisive and preferred to remain silent. A good number of 80 percent believe that expectations from patients are growing and to improve the quality of services is morally bound duty of all concerned (Table 5.42). Enriching the service profile can undoubtedly be attained by the inclusion of specialist doctors.

For example, women patients would be at ease with a lady doctor and if given a choice would prefer a lady to receive medical treatment from. Survey also indicated that tribal ladies visited health care centers more frequently than their male counterparts may be for themselves or their children. Availability of specialist's services would undoubtedly instill more confidence in tribal women and cast a great influence on tribal society as a whole. The concept of service quality is perceived with the presence of well trained and specialist doctors in general. Although it is unreasonable to expect all the specialists in a rural health care center, a periodic visit by them will help tribals perceive on up gradation process and remove the sense of long perceived alienation.

Table – 5.43 : Demographic details of the tribals in the study

		Male No	%	Female No	%	Total No	%
Age	<30 Yrs	38	25.9	59	38.6	97	32.3
	31-60	92	62.6	78	51	170	56.7
	>61 Yrs	17	11.6	16	10.5	33	11
	Total	147	100	153	100	300	100
Education	No Schooling	50	34	75	49	125	41.7
	Primary	77	52.4	71	46.4	148	49.3
	Higher Primary	17	11.6	7	4.6	24	8
	High School	2	1.4	0	0	2	0.7
	SSLC Pass	1	0.7	0	0	1	0.3
	Total	147		153		300	
Family Composition	Husband and Wife	9	6.1	9	5.9	18	6
	Husband wife and children	114	77.6	111	72.5	225	75
	Family with disabled dependent	13	8.8	14	9.2	27	9
	Family with Aged parents	5	3.4	4	2.6	9	3
	Widow/Widower	6	4.1	15	9.8	21	7
	Total	147	100	153	100	300	100

Table – 5.44 : Sample details of the Tribals in the study

Place	Hobli	Taluk	District	State	No of Adult Samples	No of Students samples	No of Health care pro-fessionals
Udbur	Antarsante	H.D.Kote	Mysore	Karnataka	36	32	7
Manche Goudan Hadi	Antarsante	H.D.Kote	Mysore	Karnataka	62	14	
Hosmala	Antarsante	H.D.Kote	Mysore	Karnataka	39	14	
Beltur	Antarsante	H.D.Kote	Mysore	Karnataka	28	11	
Badaga Matkeri	Kandalike	H.D.Kote	Mysore	Karnataka	85	55	8
Tannirkuli	Hegde	Kumta	Uttar Kannada	Karnataka	40	41	5
Dubare	Nanjaraypatna	Virajpet	Mercara	Karnataka	10	33	15
Total					300	200	35

SUMMARY OF FINDINGS AND SUGGESTIONS

The study has been conducted in the districts of Mysore, Kodagu and the coastal district of Uttar Kannada in Karnataka. Tribals in Taluks of H.D. Kote (Mysore), Virajpet (Kodagu) and Kumta (Uttar Kannada) were enrolled in the study. The findings are presented on the basis of the objectives and hypotheses set for the study.

The questionnaire was administered separately to 535 sample respondents. Sample was further segregated into tribal adults, health care professionals serving in health care centers in tribal belts and school going tribal children.

Total sample of tribal adults covered under the study was 300 out of which 147 were male and 153 female. Among the sample members majority of them were in the middle age that was between 31 to 60 years, followed by 32.3 percent below 30 years and 11 percent in age group of above 60 years. Among the sample members there were no graduates or postgraduates. 49.3 percent had completed primary school education and 41.7 did not go to school at all. Only 0.3 percent of sample tribals had passed tenth standard.

Total number of health care professionals included in the study was 35. There was an inherent limitation with regard to samples of health care professionals as the number of health care centers in and around tribal areas is very small.

Total sample of school going tribal children was 200, out of which 97 were boys and 103 were girls. Tribal schoolteachers were interviewed on behalf of children.

The findings of the research are listed below:

- Among the tribal samples 24.3 percent of the tribal patients chose to visit only the tribal doctors to seek medical advice at the time of their sickness. But, almost an equal number of respondents 22.3 percent said that they would like to go to government hospital only and 53.3 percent of the respondents were indecisive and said that they would seek medical advice from both tribal and government health professionals.

- The study showed that tribal medicine is still predominantly practised in tribal society. Almost half of the respondents are not averse to visit tribal doctors for the medical treatment. But respondents from younger age group of tribal were decisive and wished to go to government hospital only.

- It was observed that primary occupation of the tribals is agriculture besides collecting forest produce. According to respondents, tribal health problems and minor injuries are common during the monsoon season. Occasional falls from the tree have also been noticed. Tribals are poor and cannot afford medical treatment when they are sick during the season. 36.3 percent of tribal patients said that work related (occupational) problems make them to seek the advice from medical professionals.

- Among the sample 33 percent said that it was sickness of children, which made them go for medical advice. Tribal mothers prefer to take their children to government health care center.

- It was observed that most of them suffer from one or the other physical ailment, as the tribals put in hard physical work during their lifetime. Most of them were suffering from chronic arthritis (Pain in Joints) and symptoms of gastric ulcers (pain in the stomach) .

- 16.7 percent of the respondents said that, home remedies, which were traditionally used, were highly effective. In all 45.4 percent of the tribal respondents opined that their traditional treatment was effective even today. 37 percent of the tribal respondent said that modern and traditional medicines were equally effective and it was not possible to prefer one to the other between the two systems of medicine. But 17.7percent among the tribal respondents from the younger age group said that the home remedies were ineffective and modern medicines were much better.

- Among the tribals who visit the health care centers, female visited the health care center more frequently compared to their male counterpart. This shows that women had to visit the health care center more often either for themselves or for their young children to seek medical advice or treatment.

- It was revealed by the study that availability of specialist's services would instill confidence in tribal women and cast a great influence on tribal society as a whole, as the presence of trained and specialist doctors in health care centers has been equated with the high service quality.

- 30.3 percent of tribals go to government hospital only when health conditions are life threatening and very serious, owing to emergencies. Emergencies generally arise from unforeseen occurrences like accidents, insect bite. Analysis of the study showed that unless the symptoms of the diseases conditions are very severe and unbearable, the tribals wish to use their own home medicine only.

- Among the respondents, 31.7 percent had reached the health care center in time and received treatment but 24.3 percent of the respondents could not reach in time. Poor practice of punctuality owing to illiteracy is also one of the contributing factors for tribal patients to reach late.

- It was revealed that the distance by road from the tribal settlements was the main reason for their not being able to reach the center in time. Transportation systems are not convenient to reach health care centers

- Most of the respondents did not have a clear picture about the working hours of the health care centers. Many of the respondents expressed that working hours in health care centers as "two hours before and after lunch".

- 39 percent tribal patients felt that distance was the prohibitive factor in their efforts to seek timely medical advice. The next hindering factor (23.3 percent) was that health care professionals were not available when they had visited the hospital.

- Female tribal patients did express displeasure on the unavailability of the health care professionals during their visit to health care center, more than their male counterparts.

- Despite government's concern and the media support, implementation and delivery of the health care programmes are poor and not in tune with ground realities.

- 29.7 percent of respondents could not receive medical treatment as doctors were not available to treat them and 9.3 percent of the respondents experienced non-availability of the medicine. There were 9 percent of the respondents who could not afford to buy the medicines from private medical stores owing to cost

- 26.3 percent of the tribal respondents opined that there was a good response and 3.7 percent of the respondents received poor response from health service staff when they visited health care centers.

- 20.3 percent of the tribal patients could avail of medical advice when they were ill. Another 27 percent of the tribal patients had received treatment but it was late and they had to suffer.

- Tribal patients would approach health care centers only on account of uncontrolled infection even after the administration of tribal medicines. Further, they may fail to buy the medicine prescribed, partly or fully and hence the delayed visit may become a futile exercise.

- 52.7 percent of the tribal respondents opined, it was necessary to have resident health care professionals with free supply of medicines.

- Tribal respondents were also conscious of the fact that medicinal equipments and drugs from private drug stores were unaffordable and there is a dearth of health care professionals, facilities and free medicine in the healthcare center.

- A small number, about 11.3 percent ,of the tribal respondents said that they wished to have the services of both tribal and professional doctors. Another 36 percent of the respondents gave the response that there should be a government hospital in the proximity with all facilities and free supply of medicines.

- There was a significant difference in the number of the health care centers, which could be approached on foot and with the help of motor vehicles. Of the available health care centers in the study area 54.3 percent of the health care centers were approachable only when a patient used transport system like bicycles, bullock cart or motor vehicles and only 5 .7 percent of them could be reached on foot and rest of them could not be reached immediately.

- It was observed in most of the cases, in tribal health care centers the service providers like doctors, nurses, and pharmacists do not stay in the hospital vicinity. Health care staffs commute from their residence located in taluka or district head quarters. During monsoon seasons commutation to the health care centers located in remote areas becomes all the more difficult. There are no frequent buses to these remote places from taluk headquarters.

- Tribal patients have very few health care centers to depend on. It can be observed that 37.1 percent health care professionals have to meet the requirements of more than 10 settlements each and 28.6 percent respondents said 5 to 10 settlements depend on them for health care services.

- At times, bureaucratic works like office administration, court duty to attend to, medico –legal cases (to report before judicial magistrate) cause delay in attending to the patients.

- Organizational reporting system of health care professionals demands monthly meeting with their superiors, in taluka head quarters and sometimes with district medical officer (DMO) in district head quarters. This is, again, a causative factor for the unavailability of a medical officer in health care centers.

- Public holidays, periodic training programmes in district headquarters, could be yet another reason for not being able to be present in health care centers

- Difficulty in reaching the health care centers due to transportation problems affects the services. Inadequate number of medical officers on one hand and unavailibity of them due to various reasons on the other hand would push the tribal patients to the state of despondency.

- Previous experience of unavailability of medical officer in health care centers makes the tribal patients to go to the nearby clinics of unqualified medical practitioners many a time.

- Health care centers are surrounded by a number of non-tribal villages also. Consequent to overcrowding of patients in out patient department (OPD) the time to be utilized by health care professionals for diagnosis of disease would be restricted. Tribal patients may not be left with enough time to exhibit the signs and describe the symptoms of the disease conditions he/she is suffering from.

- 68 percent of health care professionals opined that facilities are poor and need urgent up- gradation as against which 31 percent of the respondents said they could manage with the existing facility. This suggests that the mere presence of a medical officer and basic infrastructure does not mean that services can be delivered efficiently and effectively. Although there has been increased outlay on the infrastructure, emphasis on effective translation into benefits for those who are targeted is missing.

- Lack of infrastructure causes a great deal of inconvenience for highly skilled health care professionals and consequently pushes them to the brink of dissatisfaction. Some of the health care professionals opined that most of the time their professional skills could not be utilized due to inadequate facilities.

- It is evident that many health care professionals are continuing with their services only out of compulsion as a result of which their dedication to work and morale will be low. This will have a negative effect on the quality of health care service delivery.

- 74.3 percent health care professionals reported that tribals turn up to them for treatment only when all other mode of treatments at their disposals are exhausted. Only 5.7 percent of the health care professionals opined that tribals came to them for the medical advice as a first choice.

- Health care professionals expressed their concern that patients do not visit the health care centers early to facilitate the treatment to be effective, timely and economical. There is a direct relationship between the early visit of patient and total cost of health care services. Health care professionals opined that effective utilization of the available health care services depends on tribal perception of quality of modern health care services and preference.

- 65.7 percent of the health care professionals felt that it is necessary to go to tribal area to address the health care needs of tribals. Only a very small percentage of respondents (2.9 percent) reported that it was not necessary to visit tribal area to treat them.

- Health care professionals opined that tribals are receptive and open to suggestions. 45.7 percent of respondents gave opinion that the tribals were very receptive and 5.7 percent said the tribals were extremely receptive. Only 11.4

percent of the respondents reported that the tribals were not receptive to the suggestions.

- Health care professionals are of the opinion that tribals of the younger age group are more open to suggestions when compared to the aged ones.

- 60 percent opined that illiteracy was the root cause for tribals being deprived of the health care benefits.34.3 percent of health care professionals suggested that it was probable that formal education could bring about changes among the tribals.

- In all, 94.3 percent of the respondents felt that education alone could make the tribal patients to appreciate the rational and scientific soundness of modern medicine and the importance of seeking early medical advice. Even within the confines of this study, education can play a pivotal role in transforming the society as health care services go beyond providing medicines and services.

- Respondents opined that inculcation of proper hygiene habits through education would go a long way in controlling the outbreak and spread of epidemics and communicable diseases. One urgent need in the rural side is to end the use of open fields as public toilets.

- An overwhelming 54.3 percent of the respondents during the survey agreed that they had a great liking for the job and to serve in a tribal area and 11.4 percent of respondents said they had a strong desire to work for the poor.

- It was observed that 65 percent of respondents derived a great deal of professional satisfaction by serving the tribals in rural areas. However, a small percentage of respondents (17 .1 percent) said that they experienced difficulty in balancing their personal need and professional expectations on account of employment of spouses, education of children, transportation facilities, poor social living etc.

- 80 percent of health care professionals agree that tribal patients get their investigations, diagnosis, treatment and medicine free of cost in the health care center. But it was also revealed that 17.1 percent of the respondents remained silent denoting that due to lack of infrastructure and manpower tribal patients cannot avail of treatment.

- But the impact of "health services for cost" could cause a demoralizing effect on the tribal psyche. Paid health services can be an independent discouraging factor for tribals and can trap them in the vicious cycle of deprivation and despair.

- A small fraction of the respondents (2.9 percent) vented their feeling that their counterparts with equal professional skills enjoyed a better standard of life in urban areas. Hence, they collect a small amount as their professional fees for the service they rendered to patients.

- A significant point to be noted is that health care centers are due for up-gradation for a long time. Decades of neglect by policy makers have virtually left the health care centers without sufficient resources. Of late, modern evolving technology considerably influences the services of hospitals. It is against this background that health care professionals in these centers are delivering reasonably decent services and are striving to accomplish the organizational goals.

- 2.9 percent of the respondents agreed that tribals accept their professional advice whole-heartedly if they volunteer to treat. Astonishingly, 60 percent of the respondents said volunteering to serve evoke a poor response and 25.7 percent of the respondents did not give their opinion. It can be emphasized here that the contours of patients –hospital relation have to undergo radical changes. Patients counseling has never been part of the treatment and integrated into health care services.

- It was observed in the study that professional satisfaction has been an important component in delivering the health care services, although overall satisfaction of patients (over all productivity) is too complex a phenomenon to be measured with any single yard- stick.

- 74.3 percent of the respondents agreed that they had been able to provide overall health care benefits to the tribal patients when the tribal patients approached health care centers.

- Nearly half of the respondents (48.6 percent) are of the opinion that Tribal patients who are victims of accidents cannot be given adequate care, either due to the late visits or due to the nature of the accidents. The diseases, which cannot be treated adequately, are contagious diseases and epidemic breakouts according to 28.6 percent and 20 percent of the respondents respectively. Modernization efforts must primarily address the facilities on one hand and its delivery on the other. In the absence of modern medical investigative facility health care professionals are handicapped to deliver the services effectively.

- Senior respondents of the health care centers observed that consequent to inadequate infrastructure facilities and limited manpower, they have to motivate the employees constantly for an effective service delivery. Seniors have to strive to mobilize the internal available resources at times of emergency. The seniors need to train and impress upon the juniors and the paramedical to enrich the behavioral profile with sympathy and empathy.

- 31.4 percent among the respondents felt that it is greatly, the late visits that deprive the tribals of the effective and timely treatment.

- Respondents were of the opinion that responsibility of developing general awareness among the tribals must be shouldered by the government as it is very essential that tribals need to be sensitized on the need of early visit to health care centers and optimizing the resources available at their disposal to meet the emergency need.

- Patients have to buy medicines from private medical shops either due to the non-availabilty of a particular medicine or for an advanced molecule.

- Respondents opined that patients turn up to them after visiting unqualified doctors in their areas and it was their helplessness due to the circumstantial pressure and poor inventory which forces them to suggest purchase of medicines from outside.

- 54.3 percent respondents said, quite a lot of patients were missing vital health care benefits. Respondents were of the opinion that a host of reasons deprive the tribal patients of many benefits.

- Organizational infrastructures were yet to develop. The poor facilities have caused a major fall in the productive efficacy of health care delivery system. Supportive activities for like health care services, like transportation, and campaign on formal education are yet to be aligned.

- 80 percent of the respondents agreed that there was a need for specialist doctors for comprehensive health care in tribal area. Only 2.9 percent of the respondents disagreed with the concept that specialist's services were needed. But a good number of respondents namely 17.1 percent remained indecisive.

- Among the school going tribal children, majority of them abstain from the school due to sickness. It was observed that 52 percent of tribal school children had an attendance between 50-80 percent and 43 percent of them had an attendance of 30-50 percent.

- Teachers assessed that sickness (34.5 percent) is the second most important reason for the tribal students to remain absent from school, next only to the discouragement factor (43.5 percent) from parents.

- During the survey, teachers of the tribal schools reported that 66.5 percent of the school children have maintained overall good health. Teachers also opined that the students who maintain good health display high levels of mental alertness. 33.5 percent of the children suffered from poor health.

- Among unhealthy students 38.8 percent of the school children were girls, who had chronic debilitating conditions like anemia, dry cough and fungal infections. Only 27.8 percent of the boys had such chronic ill health.

- Teachers assessed that 46.5 percent of the school children had potbelly, which could be mostly attributed to untreated worm infections. Physiological symptoms of potbelly were apparent. A diet of low protein and worm infection will hamper physical growth. Fungal infection was observed in 11 percent of the children.

- Among sick school children 38 percent did not go to seek treatment, instead took home remedies. Among those who did not go to health clinics 34 percent were girls.79.5 percent of the School children did not undergo any medical investigations and just had received symptomatic treatment.

- 97 percent of the school children who visited the hospital had no medical records with them at all. Therefore it is difficult for the service providers to follow up properly.

In view of the findings enumerated above an attempt has been made to compare the inferences drawn with hypotheses set for the purpose of this research.

The first hypothesis was that **"Better health care infrastructure results in better health care services delivery"**. An overall summary of the findings reveals that despite a perceptible improvement in the infrastructural facility, owing to many other reasons, the quality of service delivery has not been improved. And hence the hypothesis is disproved. The second hypothesis was **"The perception of quality in health care services delivery are negatively associated among health care professionals and Tribals"**. During the study it was observed that there was a considerable perceptual gap of the health care services delivery between the tribals and the service providers. Most of the services providers have exhibited a social commitment and highlighted the delivery of quality services where as the tribals have a strong and negative opinion about the quality of services due to non-availability of staff and medicines. Hence, there is a service gap between these two groups. Hence the hypothesis was proved. Third hypothesis was **"There is an inadequate knowledge about the merits of modern health care system among tribals"**was supported by the findings of the research. As the survey revealed the fact that a considerable size of the respondents were unaware of the government schemes and the available health care facilities at their disposal. The fourth hypothesis **"The lack of communication between health care professionals and tribals has resulted in ineffective delivery of the benefits of the modern health care system"** is supported by the survey findings. The survey revealed that there is a communication gap due to unawareness of Government schemes, inability to reach and interact with the service providers, illiteracy and ignorance to understand and appreciate the modern health care and its delivery. The fifth hypothesis **"The sense of accomplishment or achievement is lower among the health care professionals serving in tribal belt"** has been supported by the findings of the survey. A sizeable number of health care professionals have developed a feeling of regret rather than accomplishment. Barring a few, most of them have indicated a low morale due to poor transportation, communication, paramedical facility, shortage of drugs and qualified technical staff. Their presence in the health care center was due to more of compulsion than commitment and hence this hypothesis also holds good. The sixth **hypothesis "School going tribal children are deprived of health care coverage which has adverse effect on their education"** has been supported. During the survey it was noticed that 69.5 percent tribal school going children had one or the other symptoms of unhealthy conditions. Only 31.5 percent of them were in good health. Among the unhealthy students 38.8 percent of them were girls who sought treatment at home rather than going to hospitals. As a result the aggravated health problems they abstain from schools. Hence this hypothesis has been proved and reminds the need for developing an effective healthcare system to ensure healthy childhood in order to develop a healthy society.

SUGGESTIONS

Effective health care service delivery assumes paramount importance in health care management system. In relation to tribal welfare, it is a continuous process of injecting newer but practical concepts in order to make the benefits of existing system reach the tribals. Following are the suggestions made on the basis of observations, discussions and the findings of the research.

Health care-

⇒ In order to meet the shortage of manpower in the critical areas of health care centers, district authorities in health care departments should be adequately authorized so that time is not lost in replacement of manpower and the work is effectively managed. Eligible candidates from near by areas can be considered for employment to facilitate the uninterrupted service.

⇒ Continuous training of paramedical staff to increases the productivity must be considered. The training must include special interpersonal relations, awareness of tribal problems that can foster a sense of belongingness. Compensation for the mobility of health staff must be considered. This will take care of cost effectiveness and designed implementation monitored and evaluated.

⇒ It is suggested to formulate a committee under the aegis of the district medical officer (DMO) at district level to design, implement, monitor and evaluate the progress of tribal health programmes. This would facilitate faster response to the need in health care centers. This committee also should be empowered to check and maintain an inventory of laboratory chemicals, medicines and hospital disposables apart from manpower resources.

⇒ Motivated healthcare professionals have to be posted in the tribal belt. It is difficult to expect health care staff to serve continuously in tribal areas due to their personal reasons and the nature of geographical locations and climatic conditions. Therefore, job rotation of employees may be considered to motivate and develop commitment among the staff.

⇒ Special wages and incentives package need to be evolved with a focus on proper promotion, housing, skill based training for the health care professionals and paramedical to enhance their competency and involvement in the job

⇒ Working in rural area be made compulsory for fresh medical graduates and students. Government agencies, NGO's and private nursing school should unite and work jointly to deliver health care services in the tribal settlements.

⇒ Present rule of serving in rural hospital for medical students has to be further strengthened. Government agencies can collaborate with nursing training colleges for cost effective nursing services

⇒ Providing treatment to cure diseases (therapeutic) is far more expensive than preventing (prophylaxis) them. Therefore a robust system must be in place for planning, organizing, developing and utilization of the resources to achieve the objective of health care for tribals.

⇒ Tribal family should be educated on importance of immunization to maintain good health; especially tribal mothers must be educated.

Education-

⇒ Education of tribal children is still an unachieved goal. Compulsory education for the children can only be achieved through encouragement and counseling the parents. Most of the time children abstain from the school due to the sickness or sickness of parents or relatives at home. Therefore, children in the school be taught the significance of good health and precautions to avoid sickness of all types. In order to motivate the slow -learning children special coaching classes be conducted and bright students be recognized and felicitated suitably.

⇒ A clean environment, a good playground and sports activities can kindle interest in school children. Both indoor and outdoor games must be encouraged. Teachers should be rewarded with special incentives to prevent discontinuation of schooling of tribal children.

⇒ Committed teachers play a major role in the transformation of any society. To attract tribal children to school, there is a need to strengthen the number of teachers in these schools. Single teacher school may be converted into multi – teacher school in a phased manner. Whenever it is possible, lady teachers who are specially trained and have an inclination to serve the cause may be appointed.

⇒ Eligible candidates from tribal areas preferably from a tribal community should be preferred for the teacher's job in a tribal area

Demographic Data-

⇒ Reliable and stable statistical data is essential to develop any policy. An independent agency has to be instituted to record the census of tribals in general and monitor the morbidity and mortality status in particular. There is a need to develop more reliable and stable statistical data. There is a shortage of medical manpower in our country. Therefore, this agency can identify the gaps and recommend to the Government, the measures for the effective utilization of available valuable manpower.

⇒ An independent agency must study the status of undernourishment. As tribals put in a lot of physical work, it is important that seasonal variations in their food intake (calories and nutrients) are studied and government should consider subsidizing essential food products as malnutrition can make tribals vulnerable to diseases and weaken their body immune system.

Government programmes-

⇒ As the tribals have to put in a lot of physical work, poor source of income is the main cause of malnutrition and the resultant health problems. Therefore government agencies must develop income-generating programmes. Their field of excellence can be identified and can be trained further under the guidance of professionals.

⇒ Government must build houses for tribal populations to provide minimum space of living and toilet facility.

⇒ The NGOs working within the tribal area be strengthened further by government. The role of NGOs in educating tribals in general and on health care in particular, be appreciated. The government must sponsor training and development programmes for the NGOs and the services of experts be made available to the tribes by facilitating the working of NGOs.

CONCLUSION

A number of factors are responsible for the tribals not being able to get the benefits of modern health care. Thc main reason is due to the geographical isolation and inaccessibility. Health care centers are far away from tribal areas and poor transportation makes it even more difficult for tribals to make use of the available medical facilities. In the tribal context, environment plays an important role in the framework and evaluation of health care systems. Therefore, policies and programmes should be evolved keeping in mind the ground realities. Poor socioeconomic condition forces the tribal children to give up their education. No doubt, existing heath care system is people centric but it is the fact that the benefits have not reached the tribals.

It was observed during the study that most of the tribal families live in thatched huts with floors made up of mixture of cow- dung and mud. Sanitation and drainage systems are poor. Malnutrition and gastrointestinal disorders are common among tribal populations. Many tribal homes have animals (goat, rabbits) and birds at home, living side by side with them. If tribals are not enlightened on the importance of clean environment at home, it may result in communicable diseases of childhood turning into chronic diseases. Protein deficiencies, which have been detected in gross amount, may aggravate disease conditions.

Absence of qualified medical practitioners have resulted in mushrooming clinics run by unqualified (quacks) medical practitioners in and around tribal areas. Use of infected syringes and needles by them may transmit infections. It was also revealed during the study that, very few of tribals were able to read and write. Therefore, they could not appreciate the benefits of modern medical facilities.

Two questions are central to understand the effects of health care service delivery system in tribal areas, one being their knowledge of the modern health care system indicating needs, interests, and preferences and the second is the accessibility to the health care center. Research reveals that media influences the knowledge, opinions, attitudes, and behaviors of target audience. Media can disseminate ideas, images, themes, and stories. Therefore, media can play a potential role by being a part of all health related promotional programmes in tribal areas. The media both the audio and the visual can play a major role in disseminating health awareness. Every Haadi (tribal village) can be provided with a radio or TV set. This provision of audio-visual media is especially important in view of the high scale of illiteracy prevailing. The department of public health also can project films relating to community and personal health at village shandys (*santhe in Kannada)* and fairs through their mobile vans. Posters can also be put up at public places. N.S.S and Seva Dal camps can also be organized in tribal areas. In this context, the yeoman service being rendered by Dr. Sudarshan for the Soligas at B.R.Hills is highly commendable.

The plans and policy options of health care delivery system should be ambitious, at the same time, be guided by the realities. At times, enthusiastic and ambitious health care delivery system has an utopian appeal. Hence, it is imperative to carry out locally relevant initiatives for better service delivery.

There is a wide scope for studying the problems inherent to the tribal society. Developing a system that can ensure a close monitoring and evaluation of the implementation of delivery system to augment positive response from the tribals is the need of the hour. Though a number of national and international agencies have conducted studies to evolve schemes for upliftment of this vulnerable section of the Indian society, every one is of the opinion that there is a mismatch between the problems and solutions. It is true that there is no single measure to correct any system but a holistic approach to the problem may lead us nearer to the goal . If an effective machinery to supervise and execute the health care services of the tribals is developed with social and legal accountability, an inseparable, historical and a sizeable section of the Indian society who have been neglected so far in the glare of modernization can be protected before it vanishes. In order to achieve national integrity in this regard a time bound and comprehensive health programme needs to be developed so as to bring prosperity and progress to our tribal brothers and sisters.

CPSIA information can be obtained
at www.ICGtesting.com
Printed in the USA
LVHW042107240323
742526LV00001B/115

9 781805 247876